The Military Alphabet

Also used by NATO and for Aviation purposes.

A-Alpha

B-Bravo

C-Charlie

D-Delta

E-Echo

F-Foxtrot

G-Golf

H-Hotel

I-India

J-Juliet

K-Kilo

L-Lima

M-Mike

N-November

O-Oscar

P-Papa

Q-Quebec

R-Romeo

S-Sierra

T-Tango

U-Uniform

V-Victor

W-Whiskey

X-X-ray

Y-Yankee

Z-Zulu

My Military Name:

example: Mary=
Mike Alpha Romeo Yankee

____

- -

____

- -

____

__Date Started:__

- - - - - - - - - - - - - -

____

__Date Finished:__

- - - - - - - - - - - - - -

____

A = ALPHA
(AL fah)

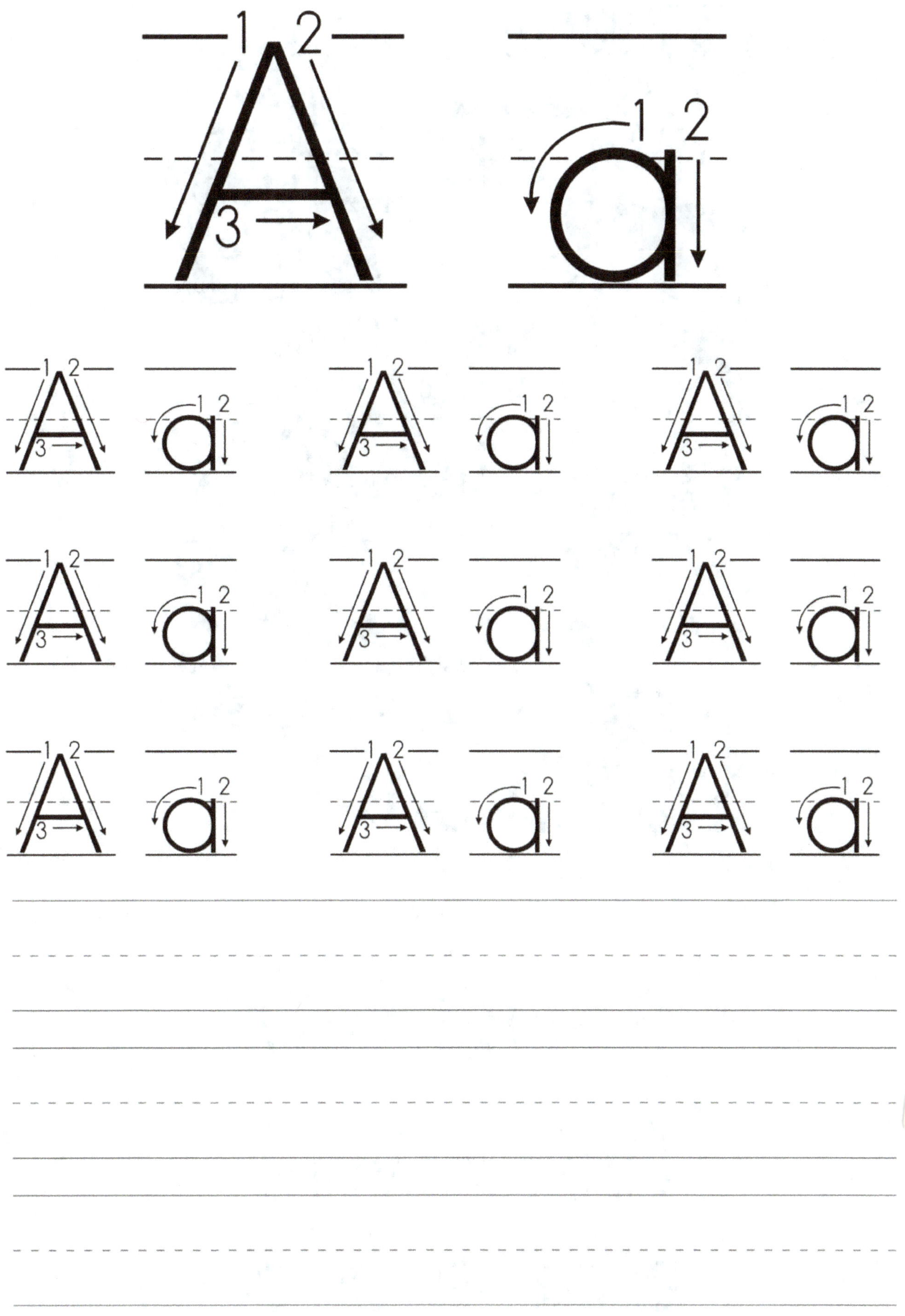

B = BRAVO
(BRAH voh)

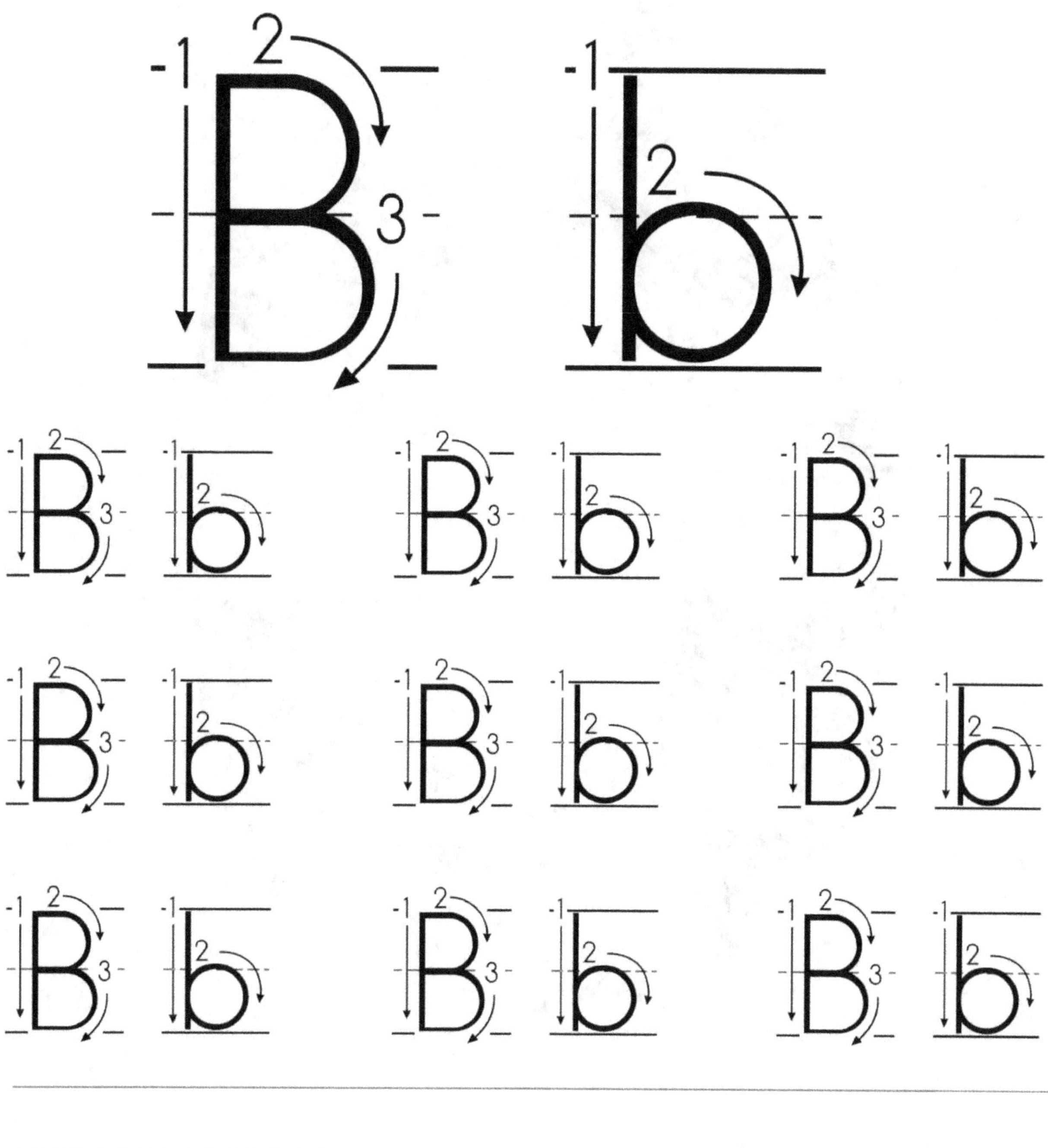

C = CHARLIE
(CHAR lee)

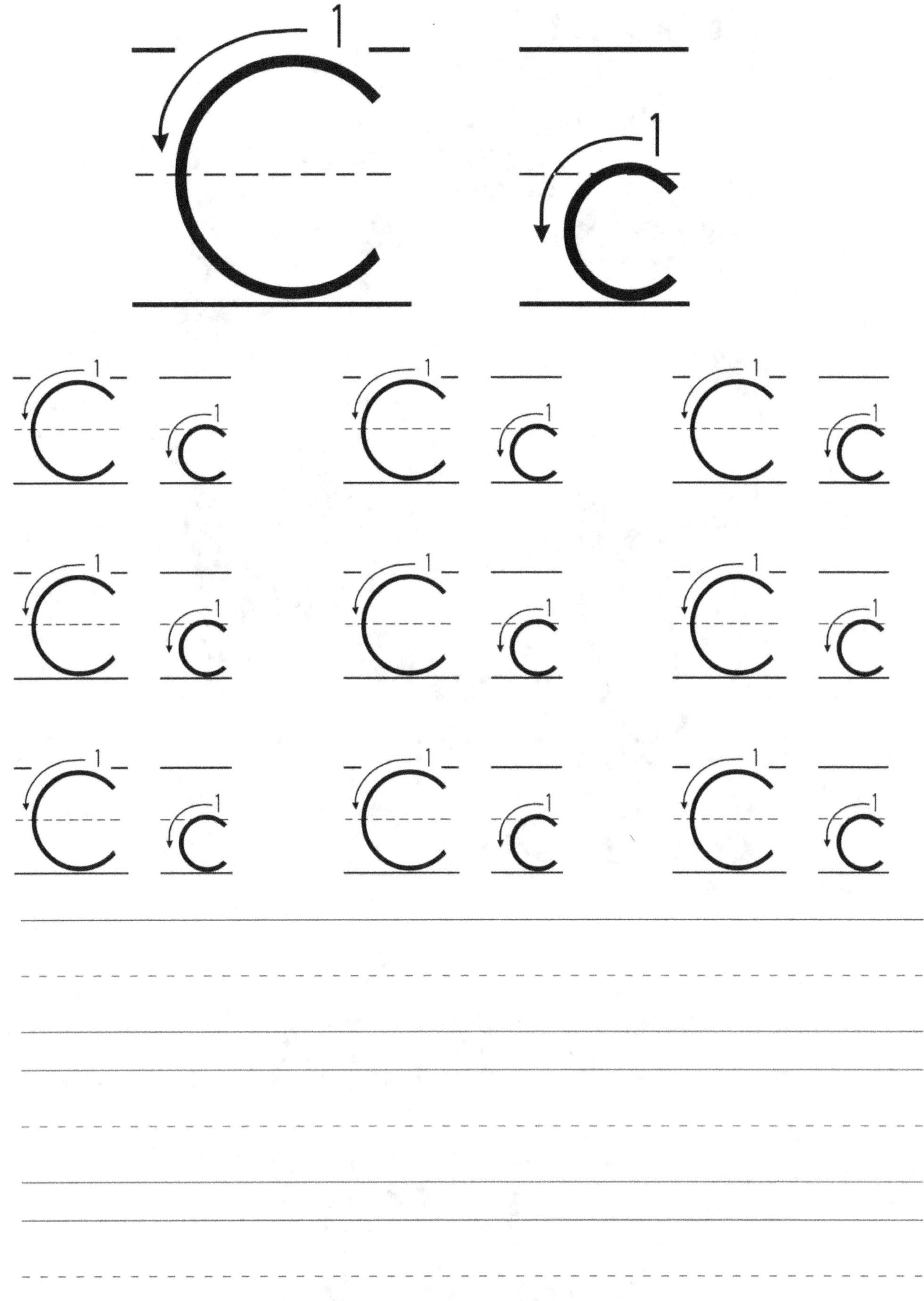

D = DELTA
(DEL tah)

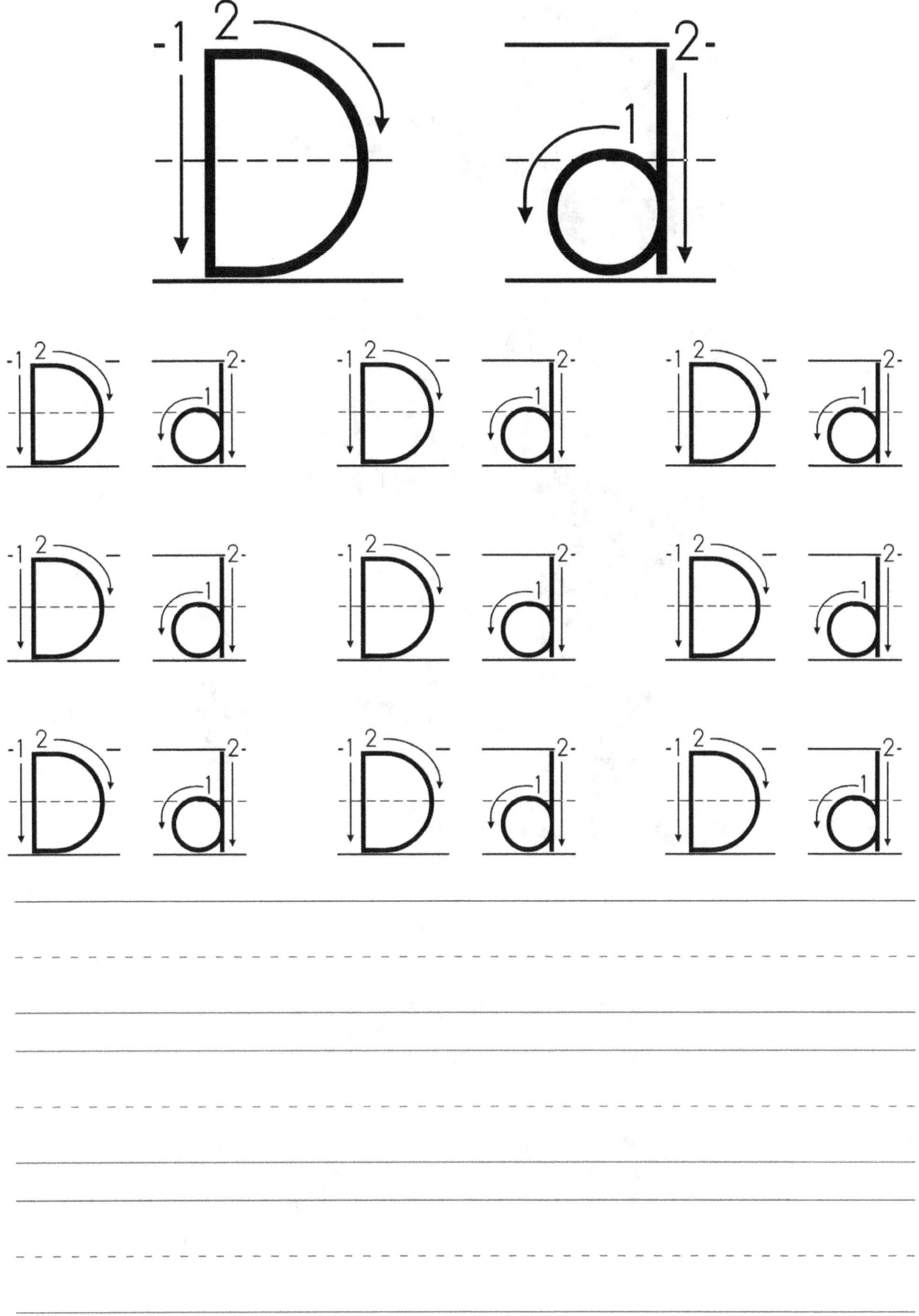

E = ECHO
(EKK OH)

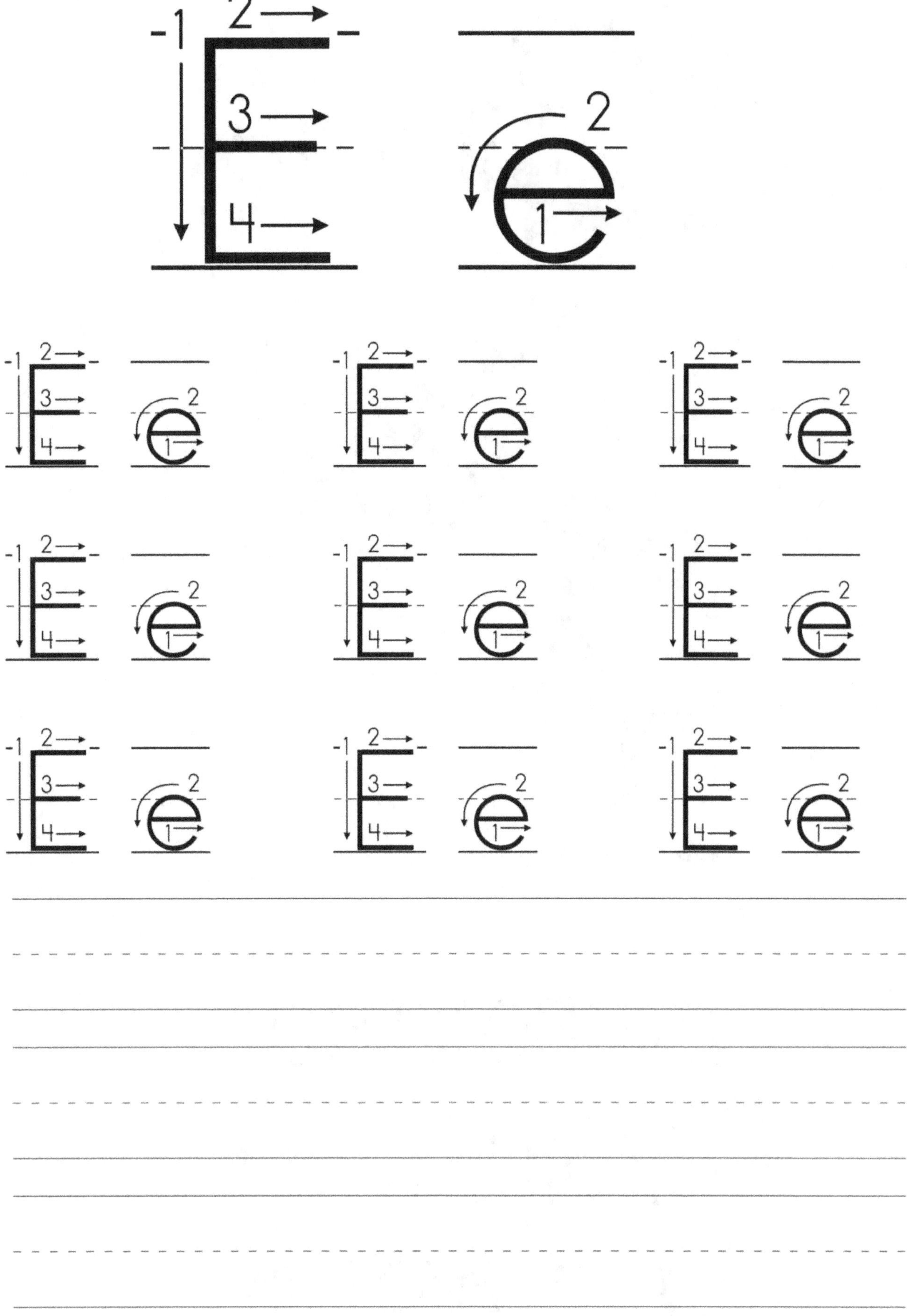

F = FOXTROT
(FOKS trot)

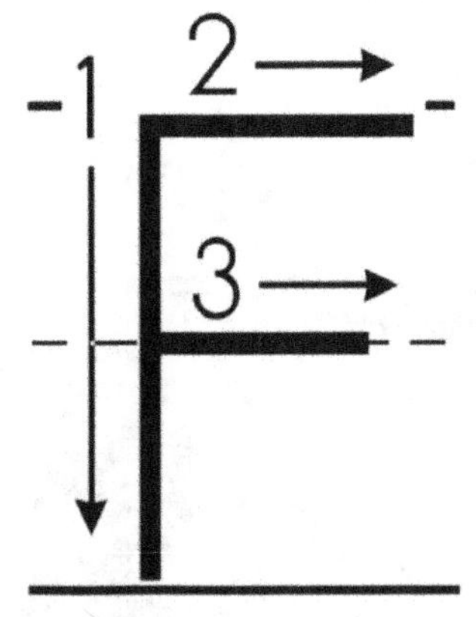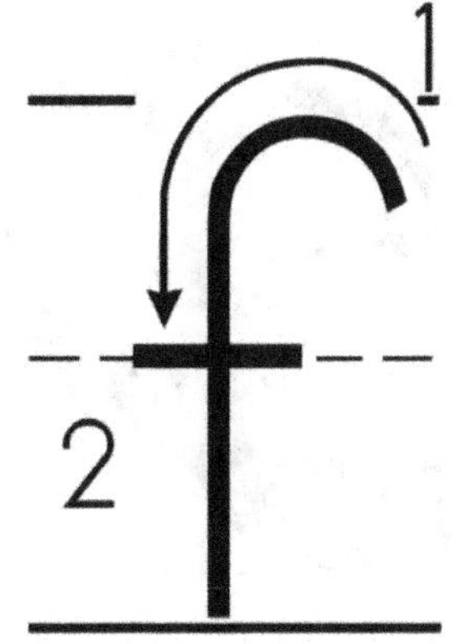

G = GOLF

(GOLF)

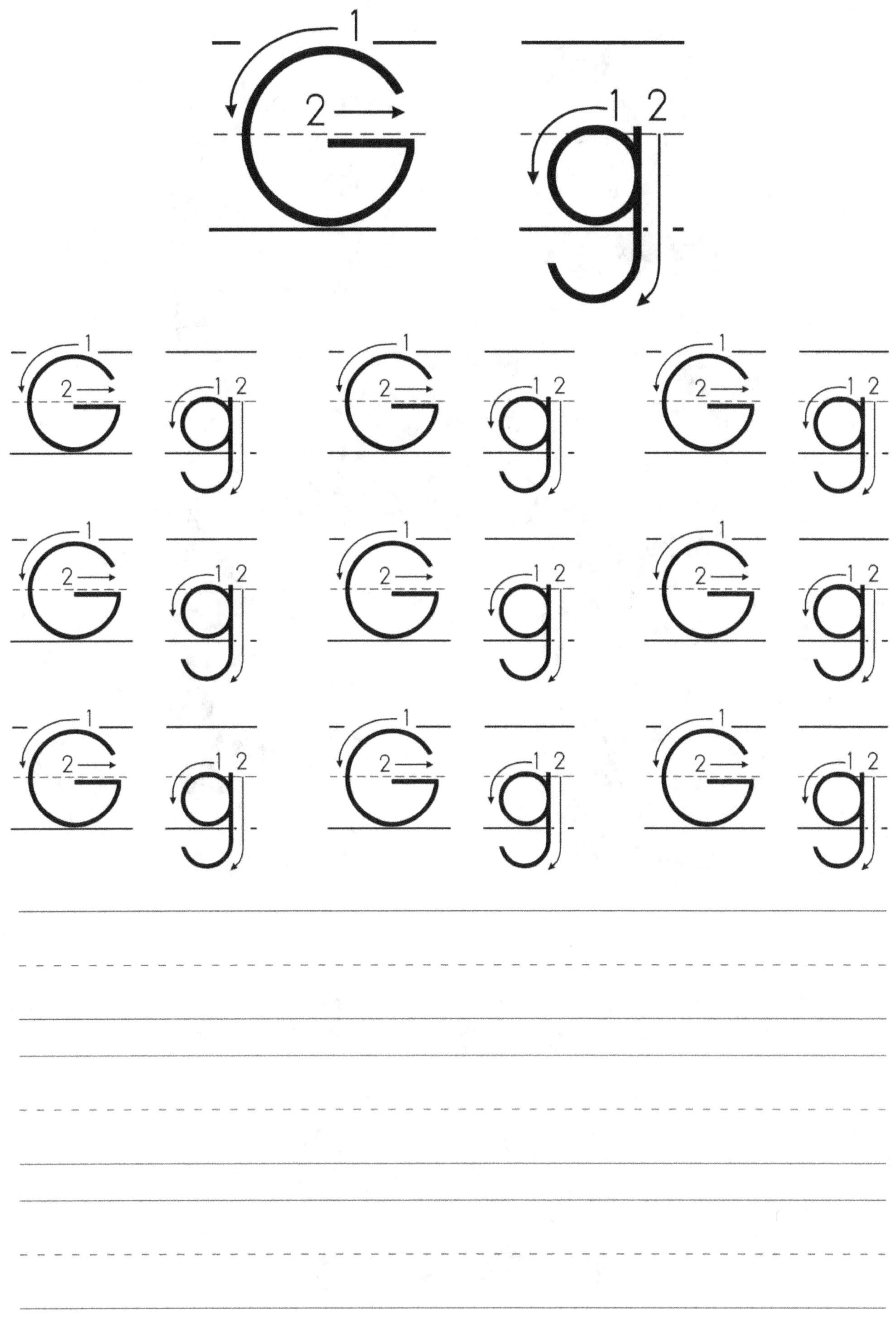

H = HOTEL

(HO tell)

● ● ● ●

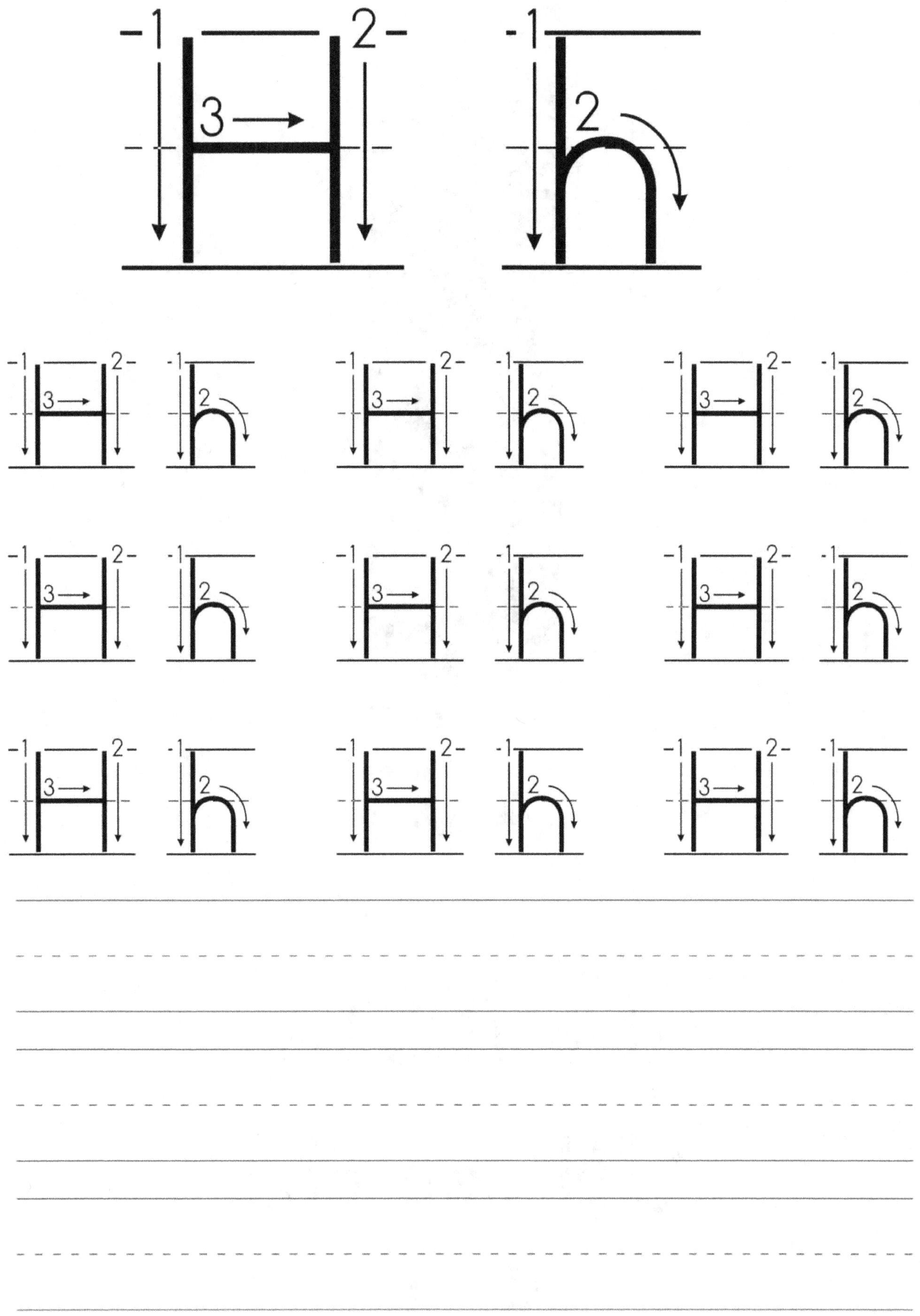

I = INDIA
(IN dee ah)

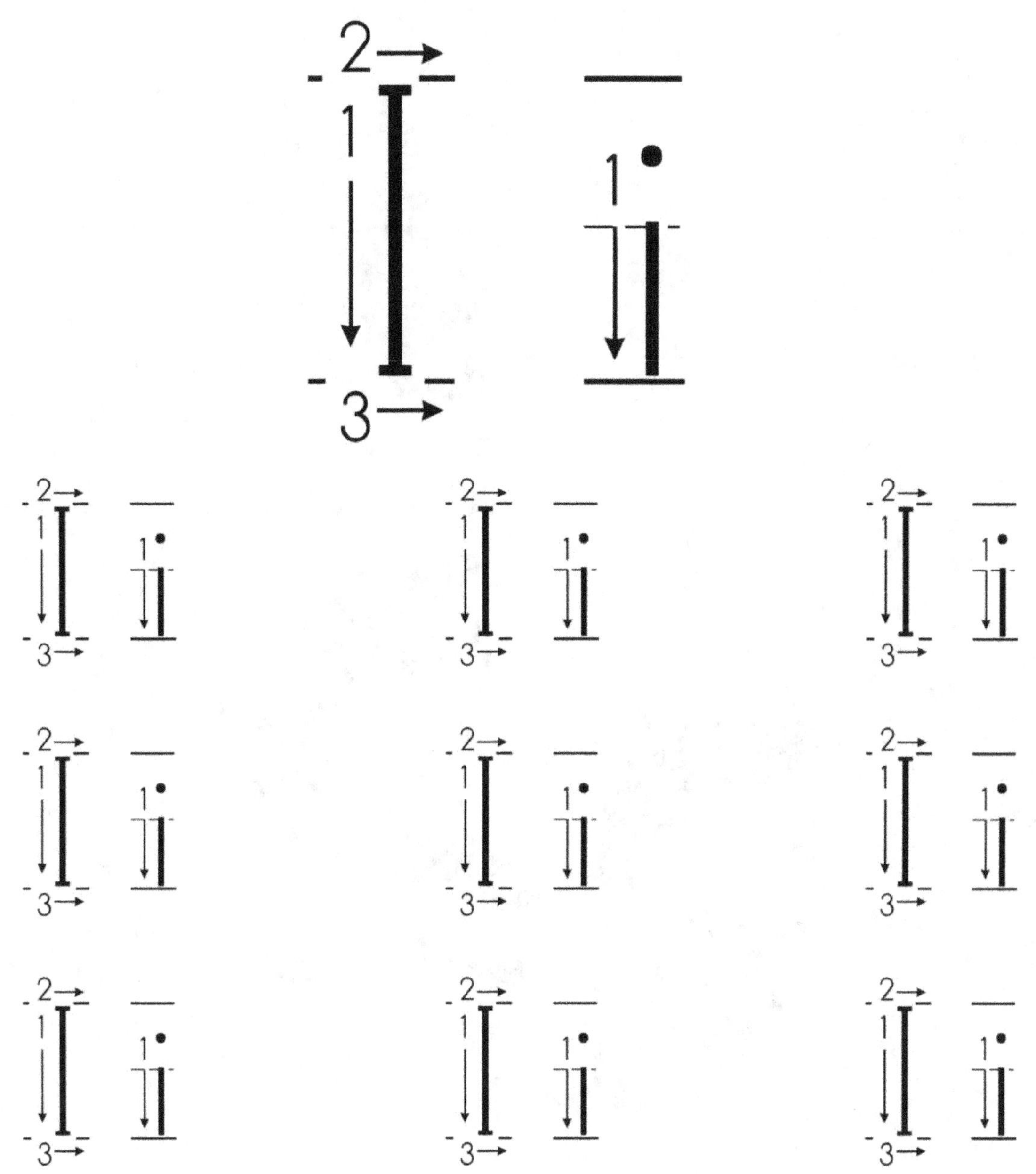

J = JULIET

(JEW lee ett)

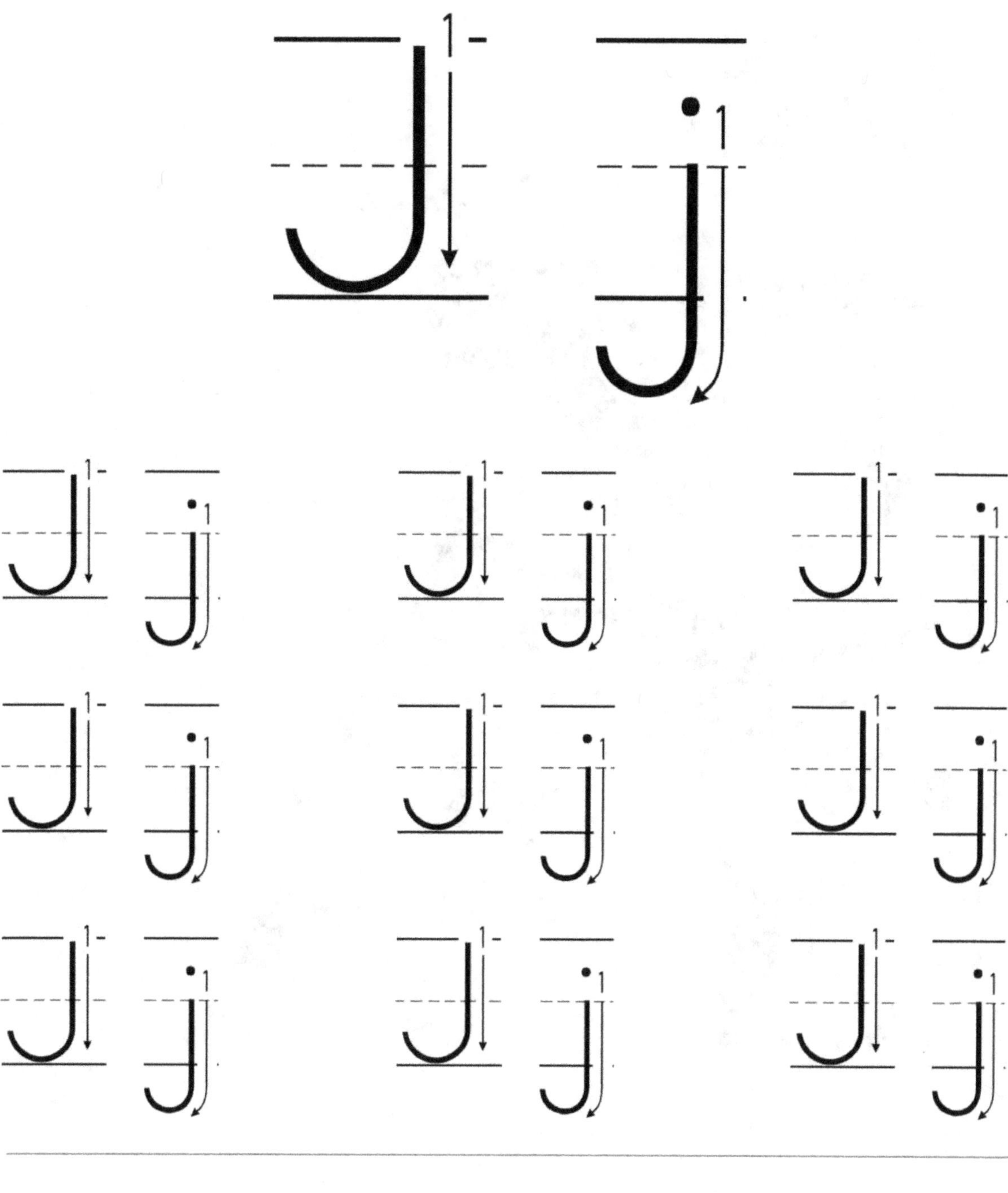

K = KILO

(KEY loh)

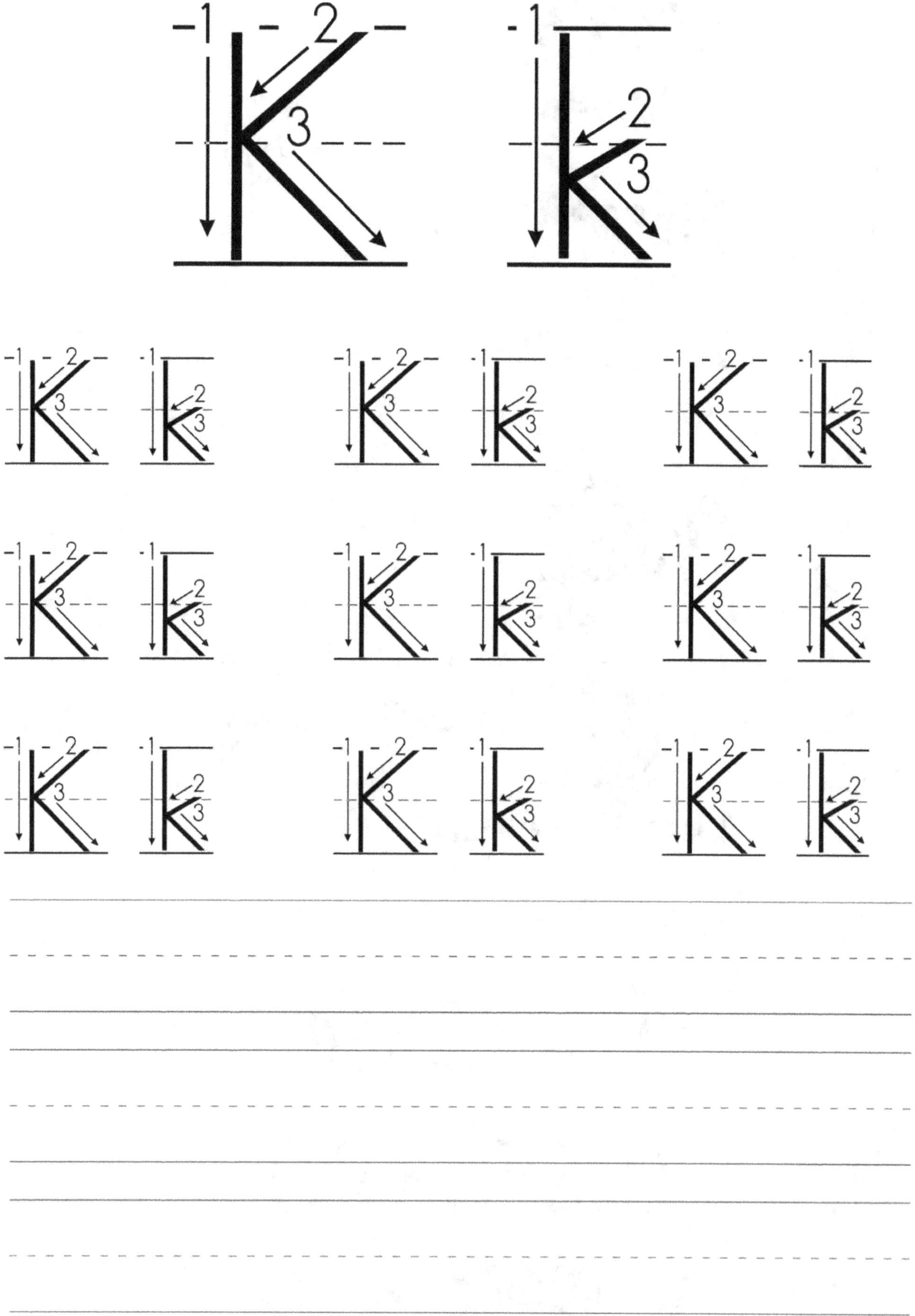

L = LIMA

(LEE mah)

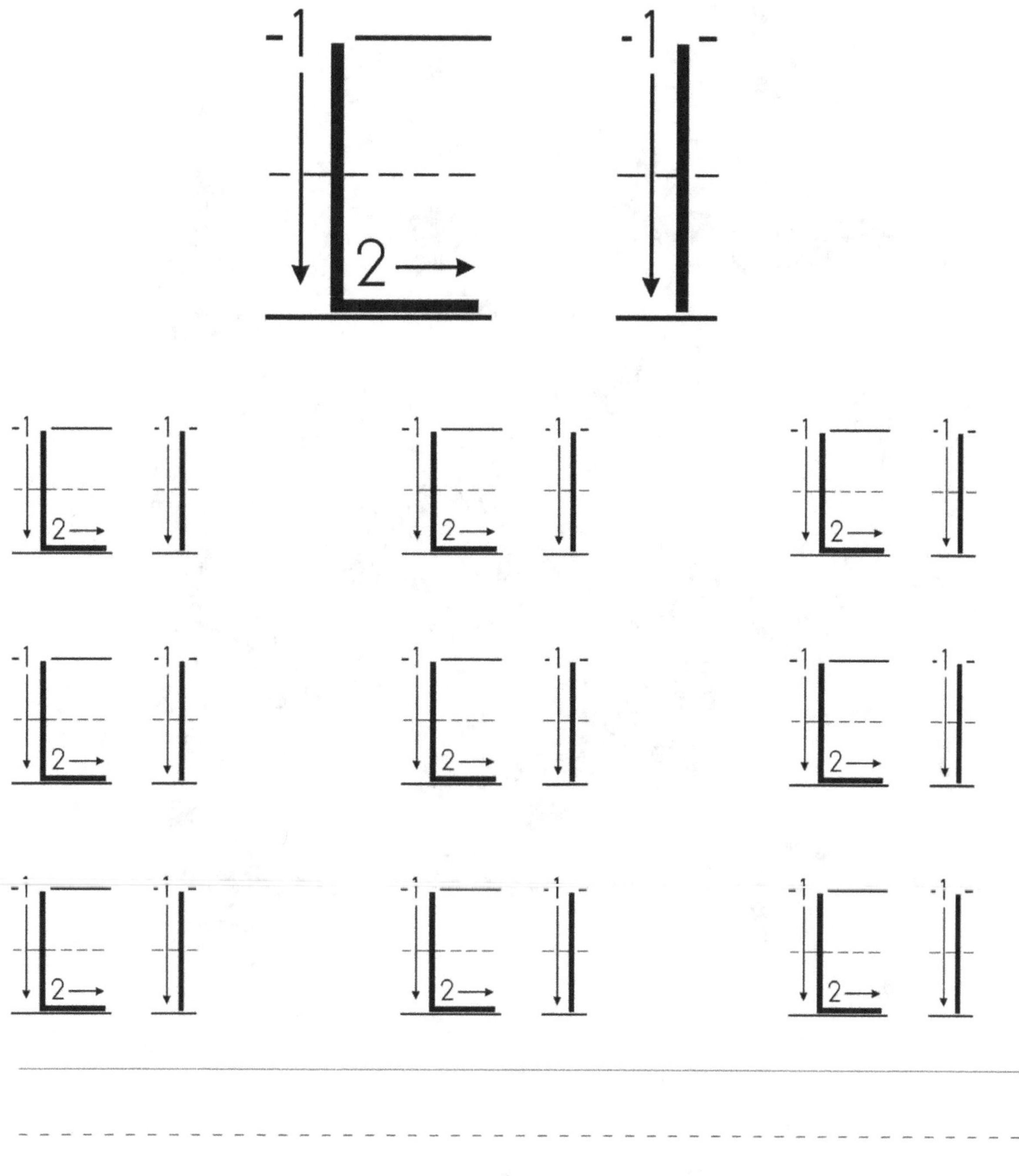

M = MIKE

(MIKE)

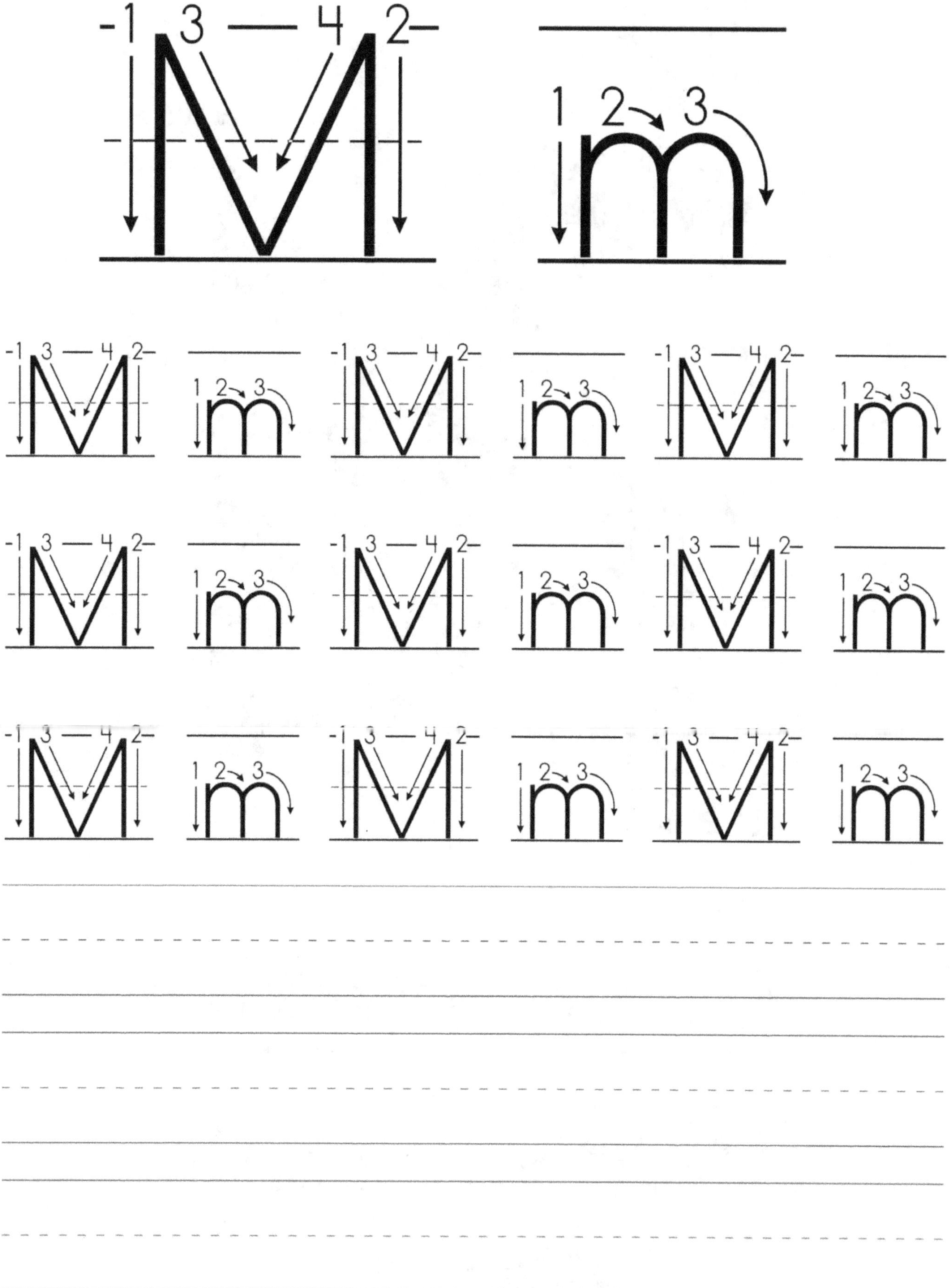

N = NOVEMBER

(NOH vem ber)

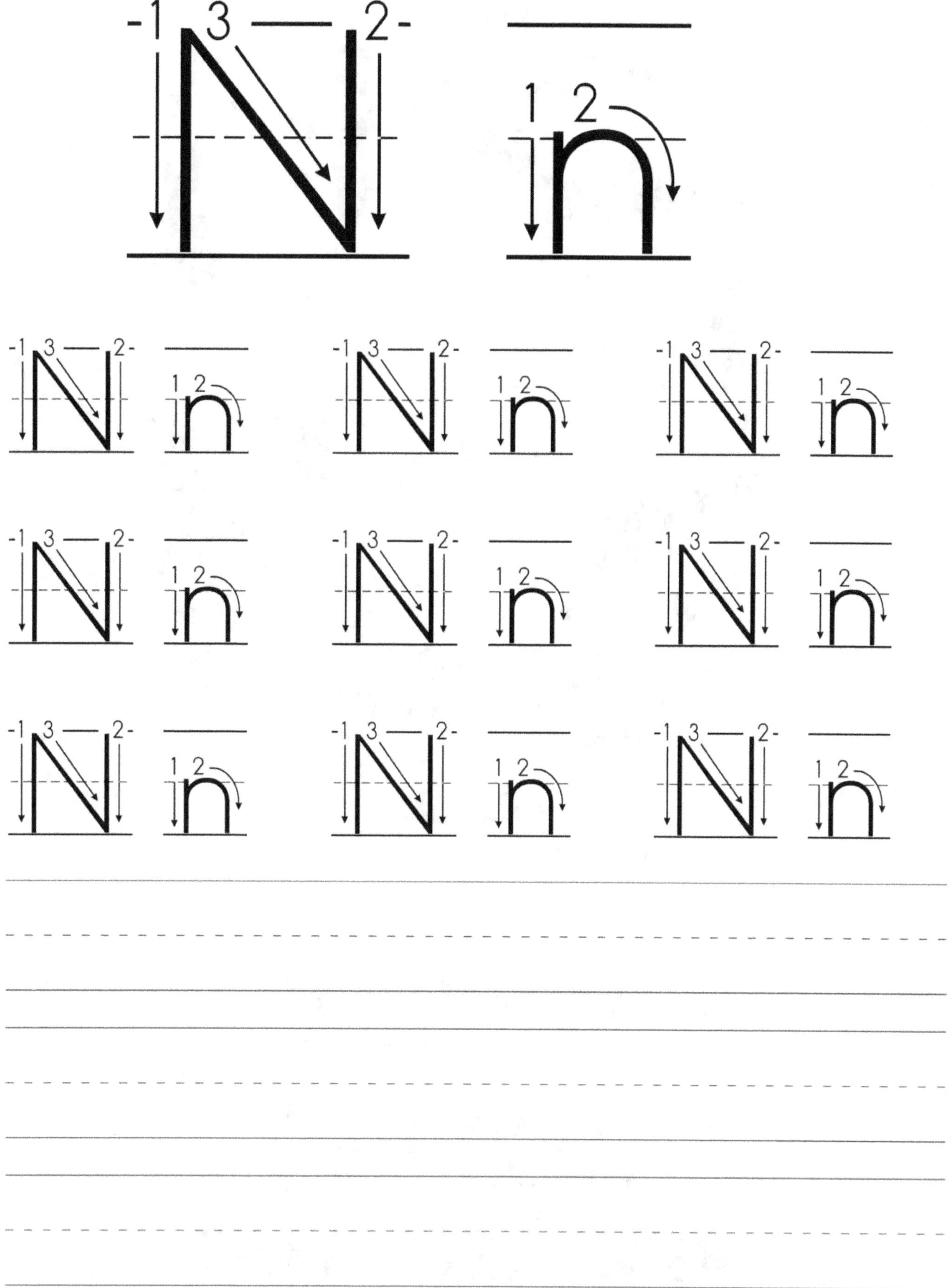

O = OSCAR

(OSS car)

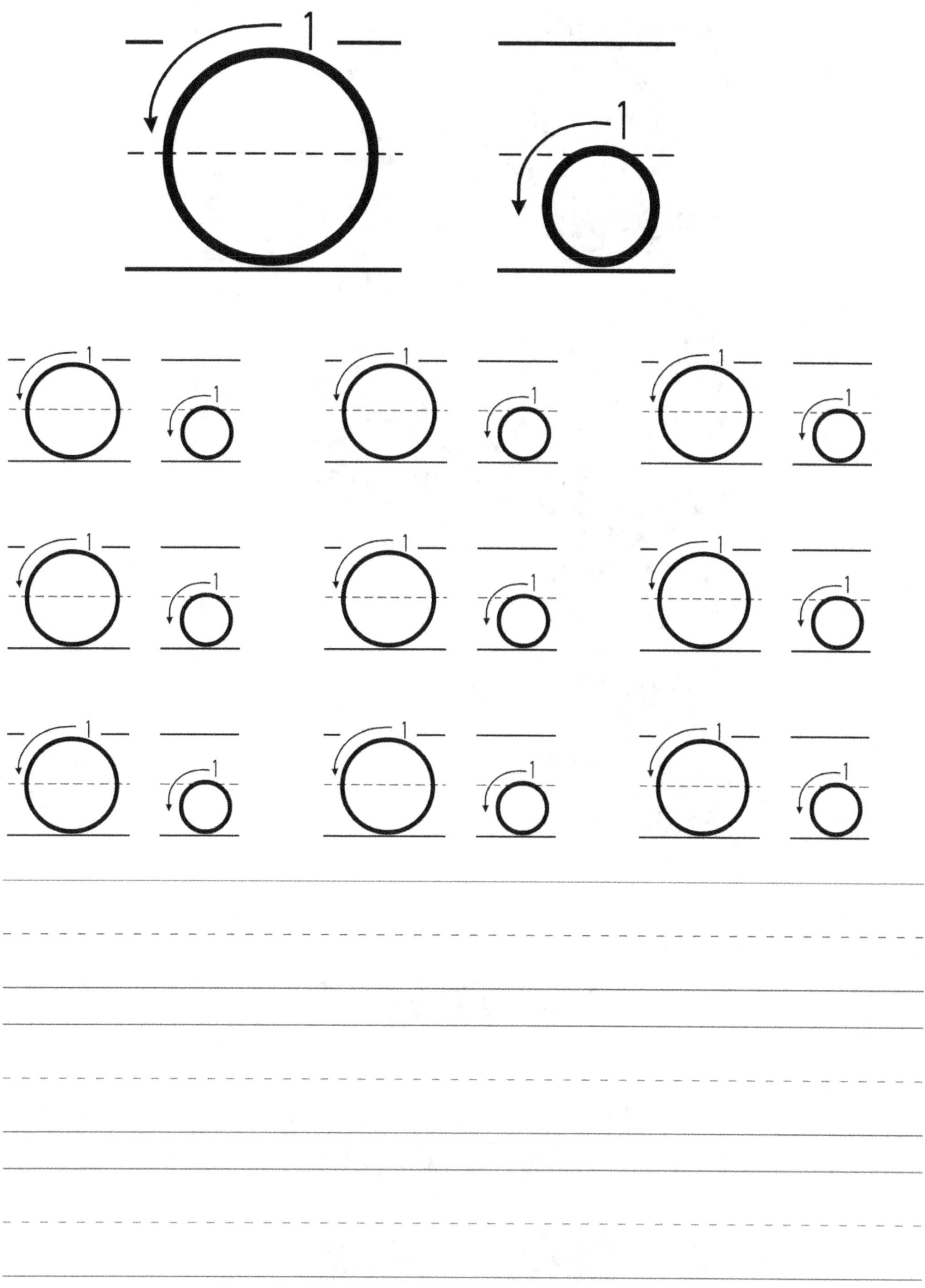

P = PAPA

(PAH pah)

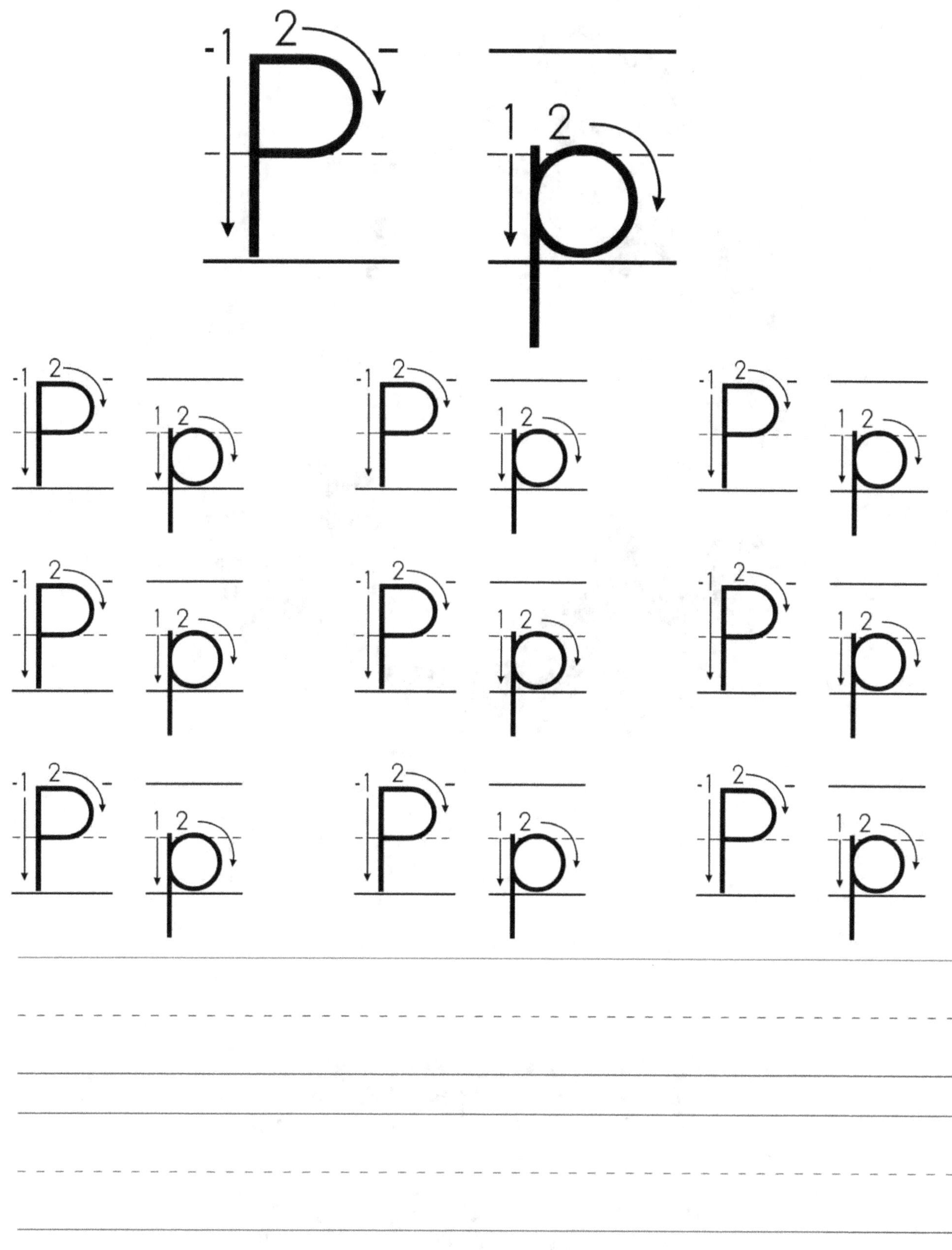

Q = QUEBEC

(keh BECK)

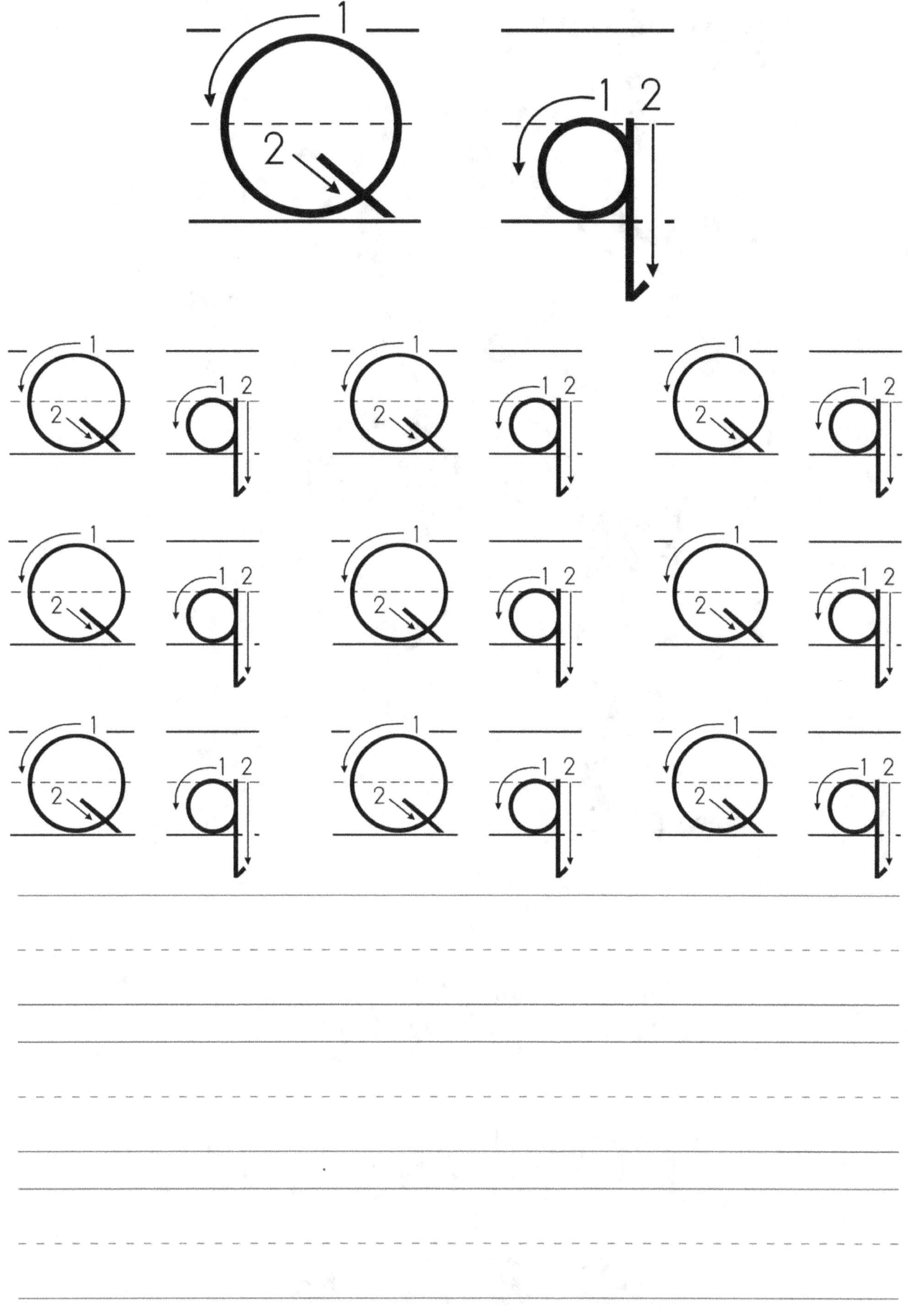

R = ROMEO
(ROW me oh)

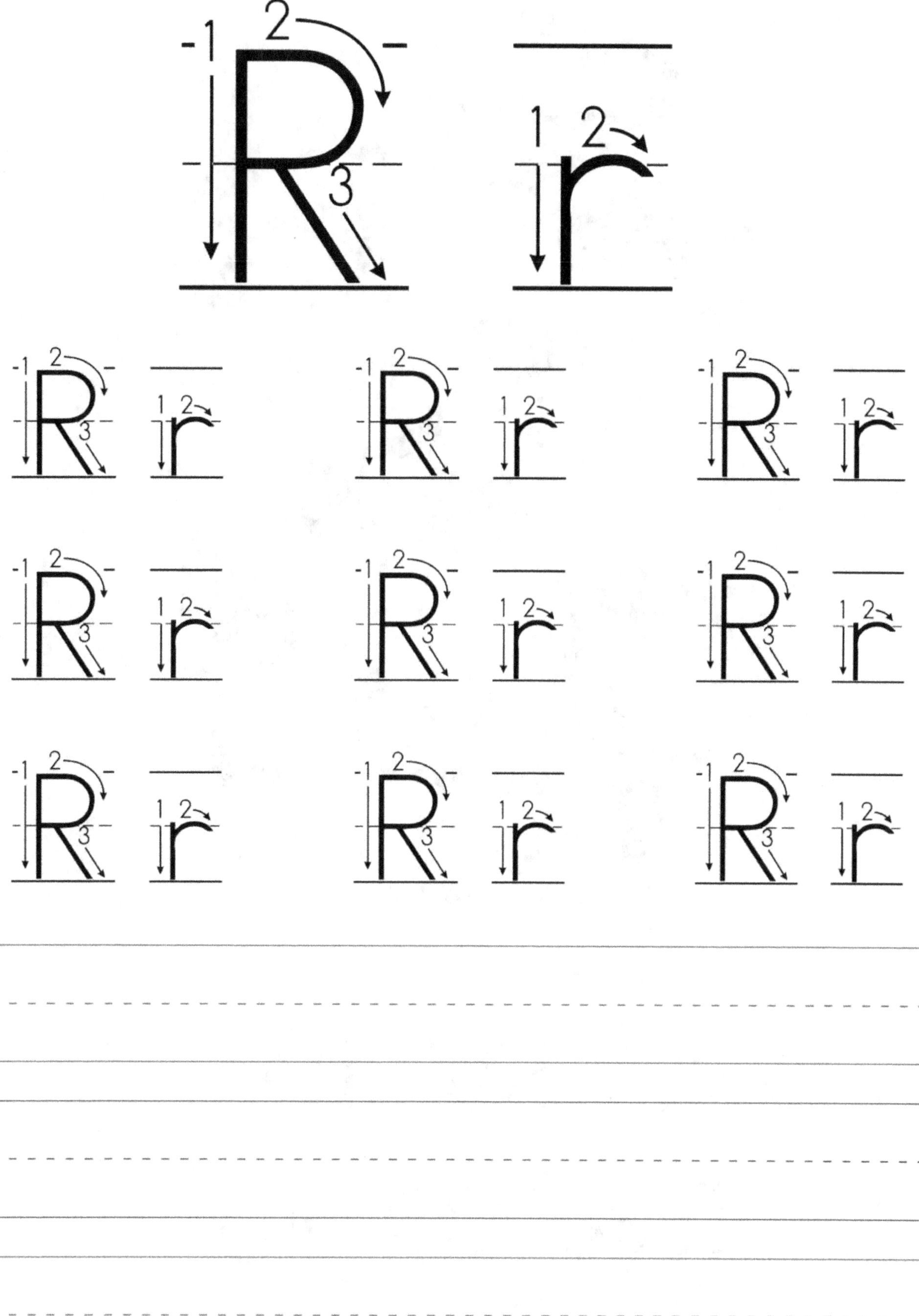

S = SIERRA

(see AIR ah)

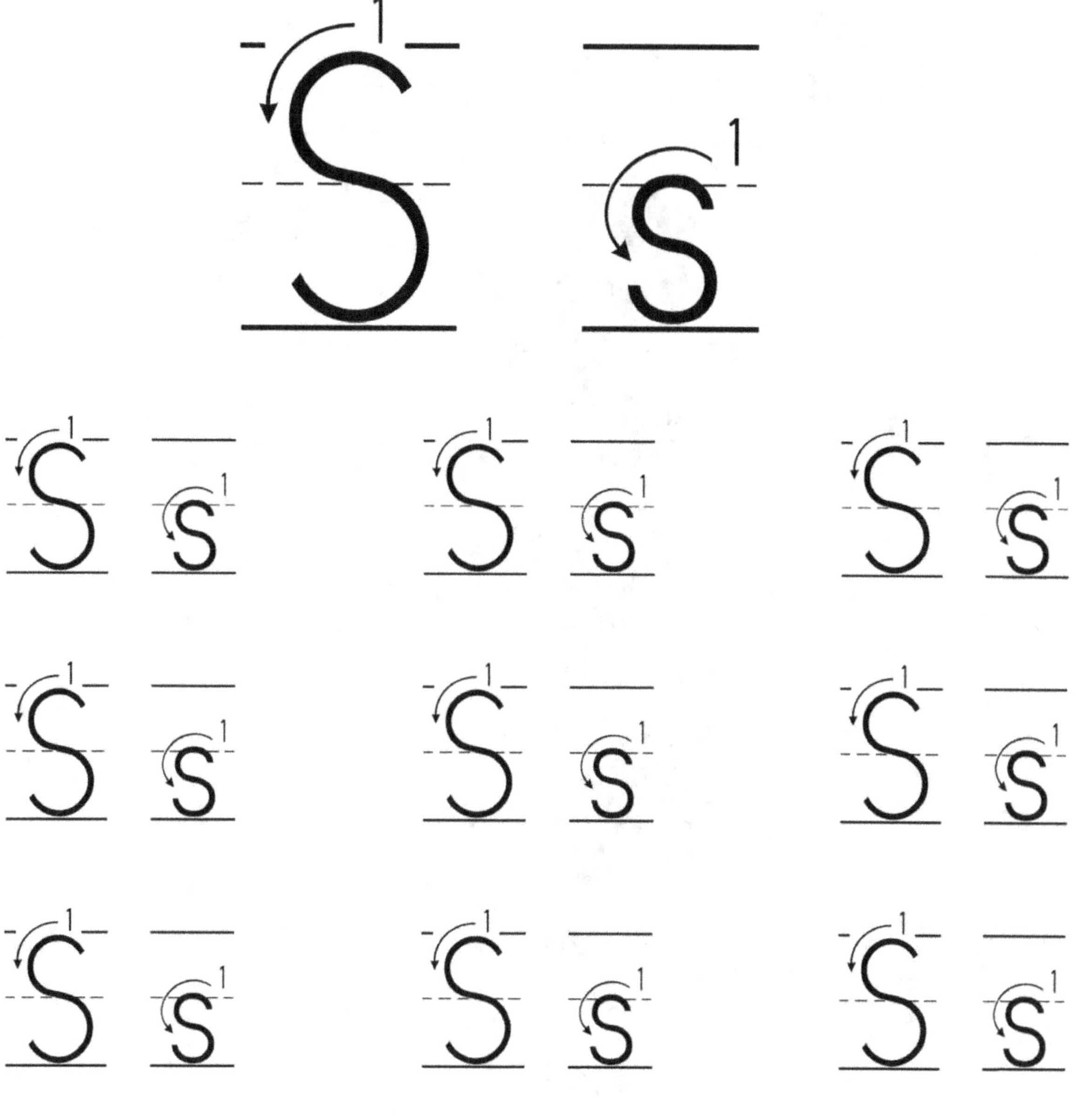

T = TANGO

(TANG go)

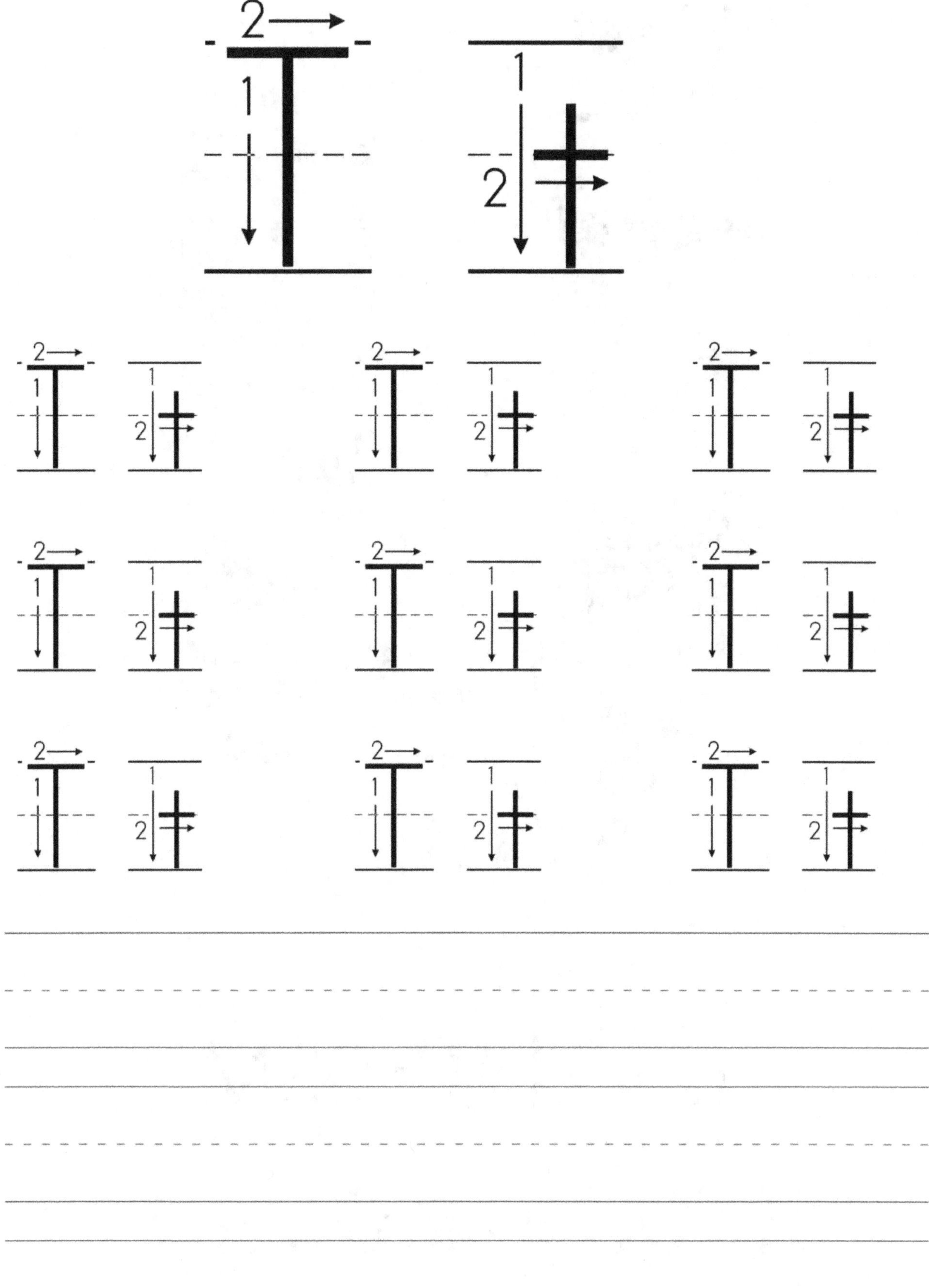

U = UNIFORM
(YOU nee form)

V = VICTOR

(VIK ter)

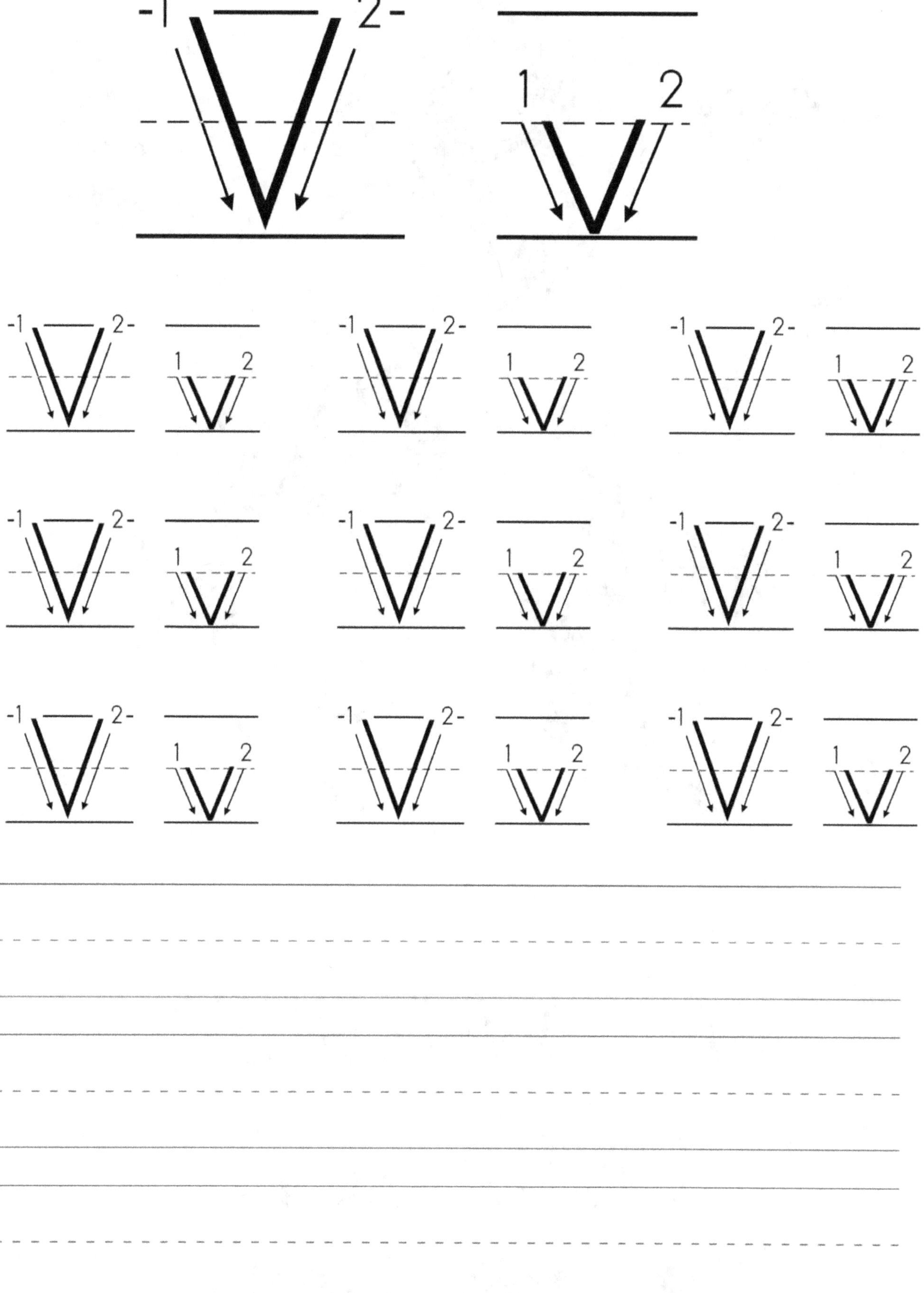

W = WHISKEY

(WISS key)

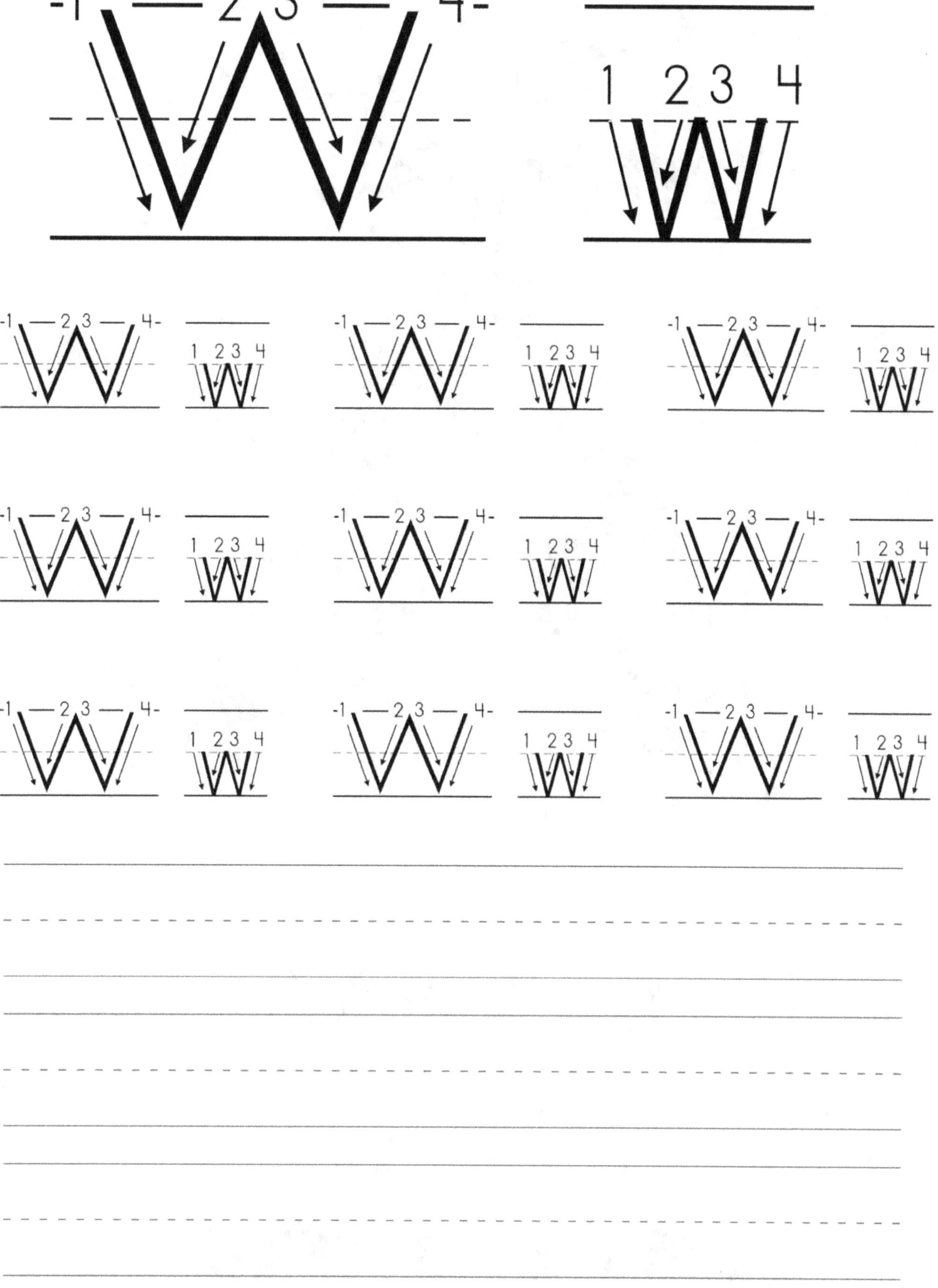

X = X-RAY

(EKS ray)

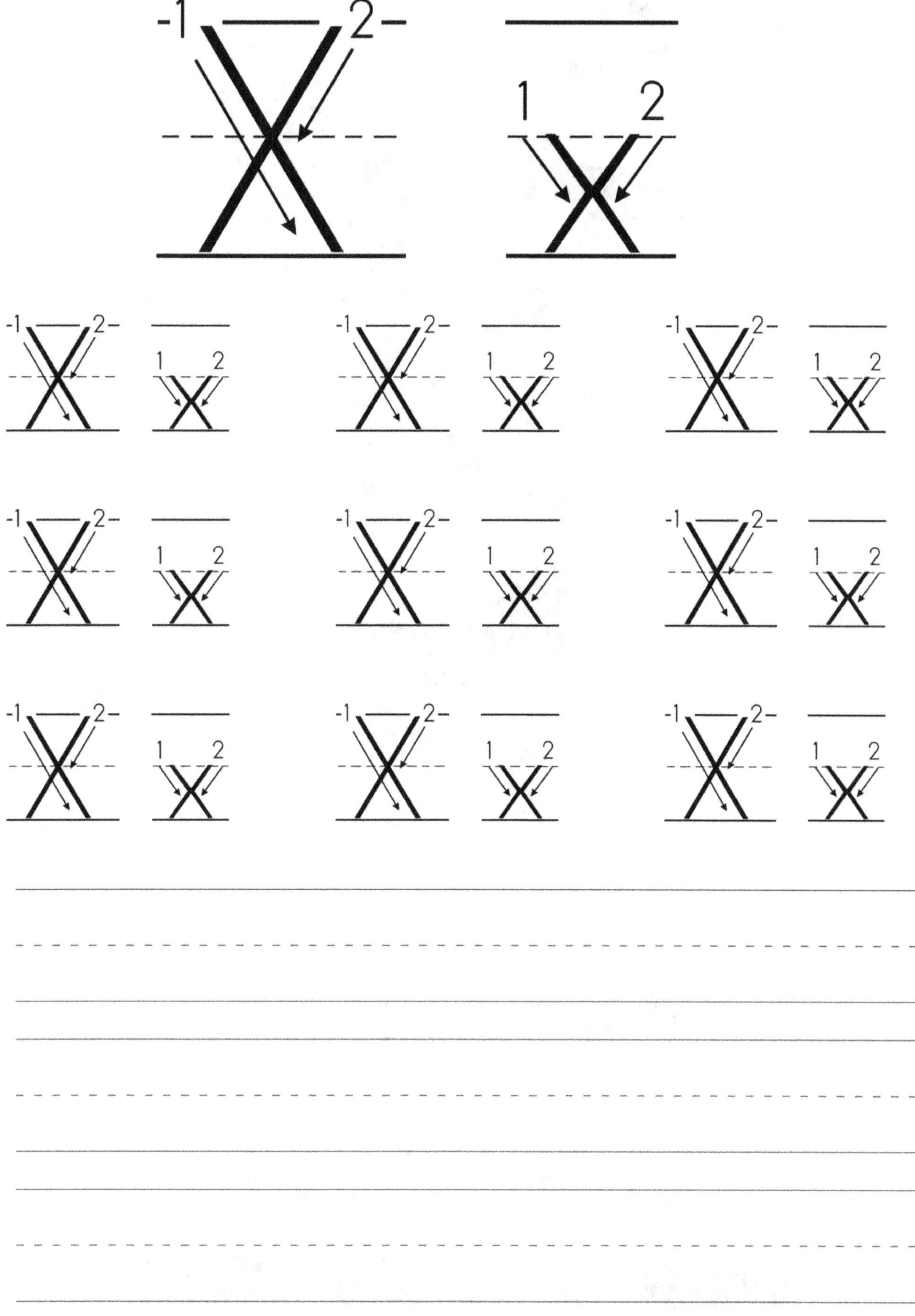

Y = YANKEE

(YANG key)

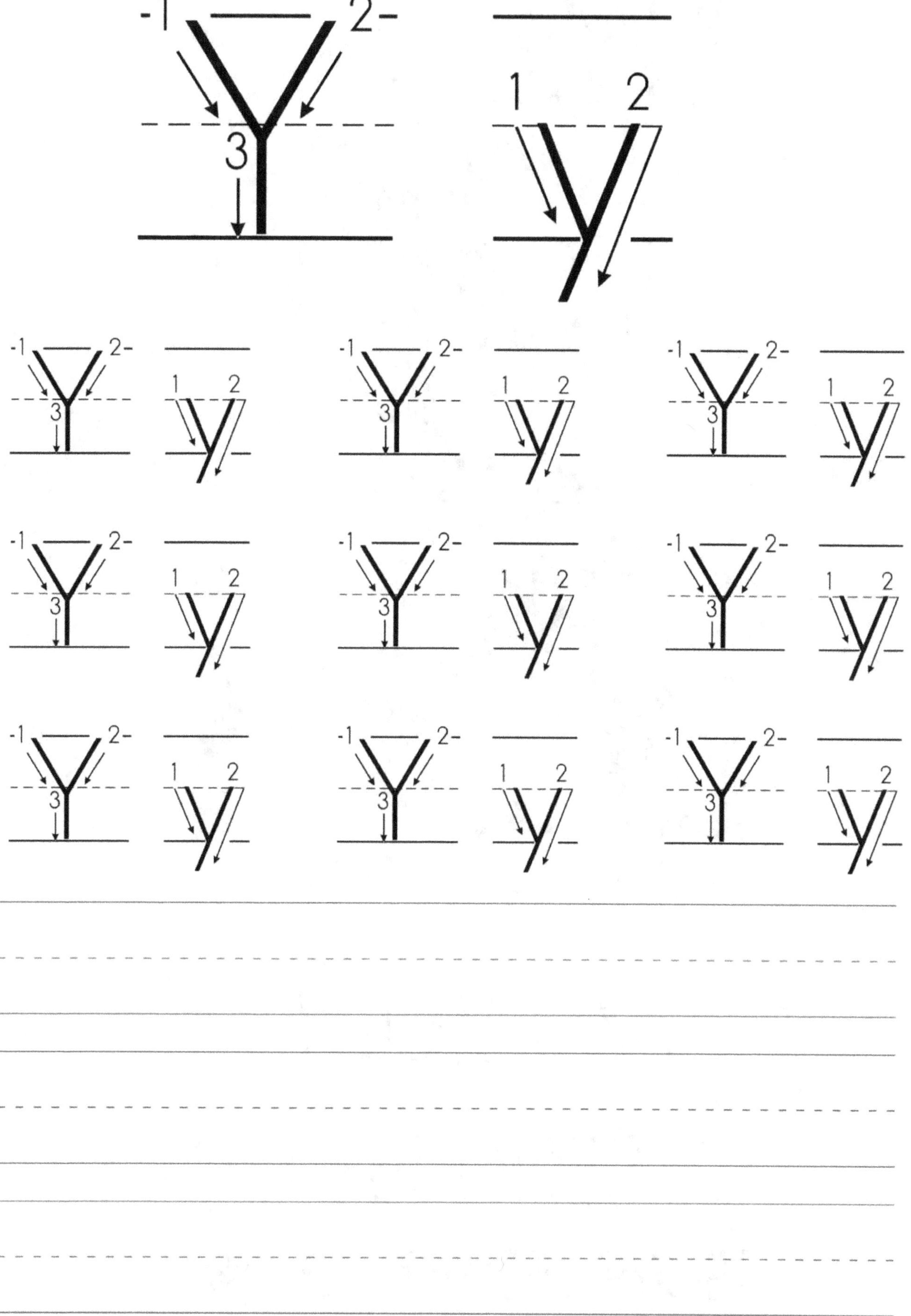

Z = ZULU
(ZOO loo)

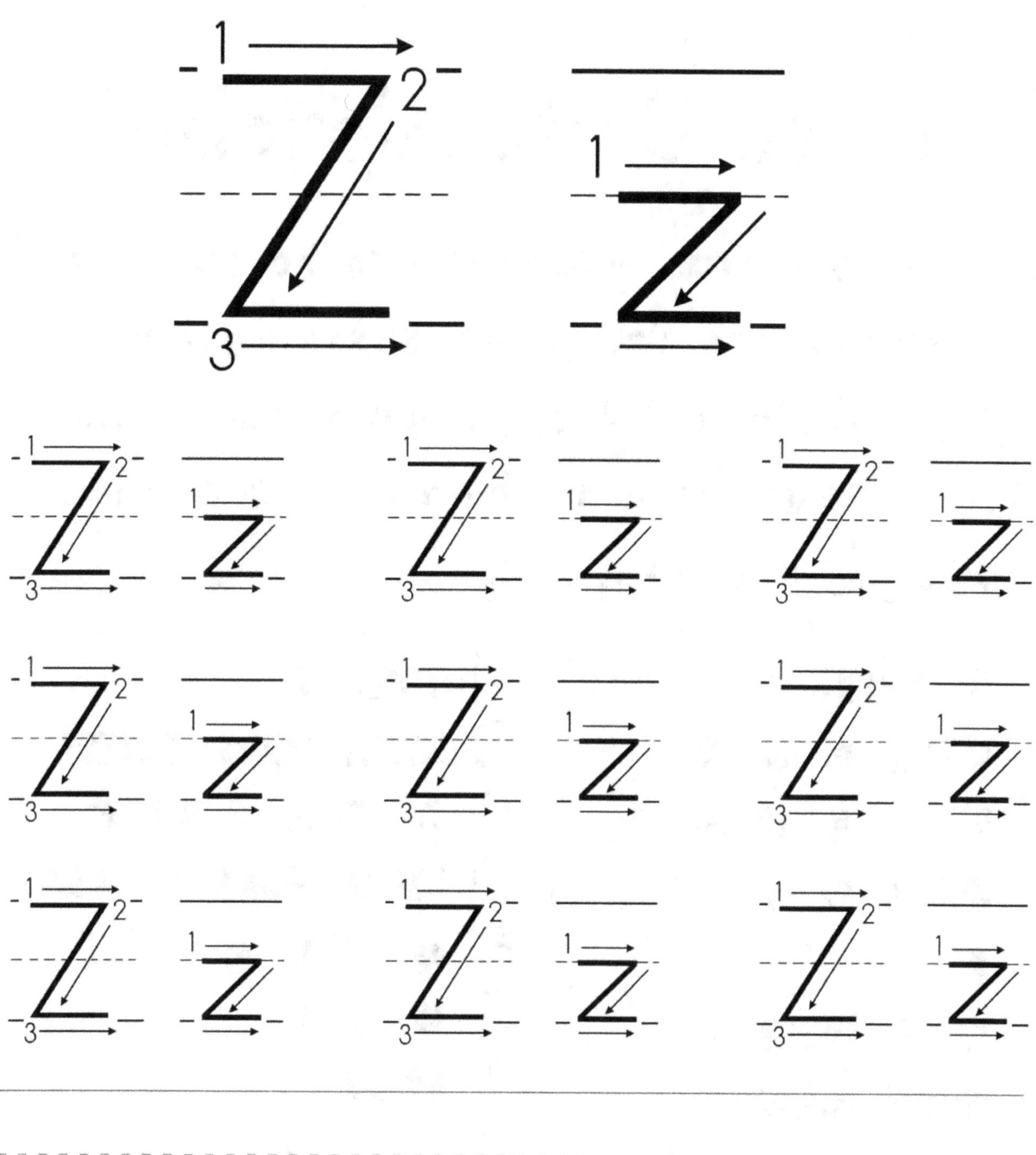

Morse Code Alphabet

   Morse code was invented around 1837 to be used for the Telegraph system (think really old phone calls). Each Morse code letter or number is formed by a sequence of dits (●) and dahs (▬).

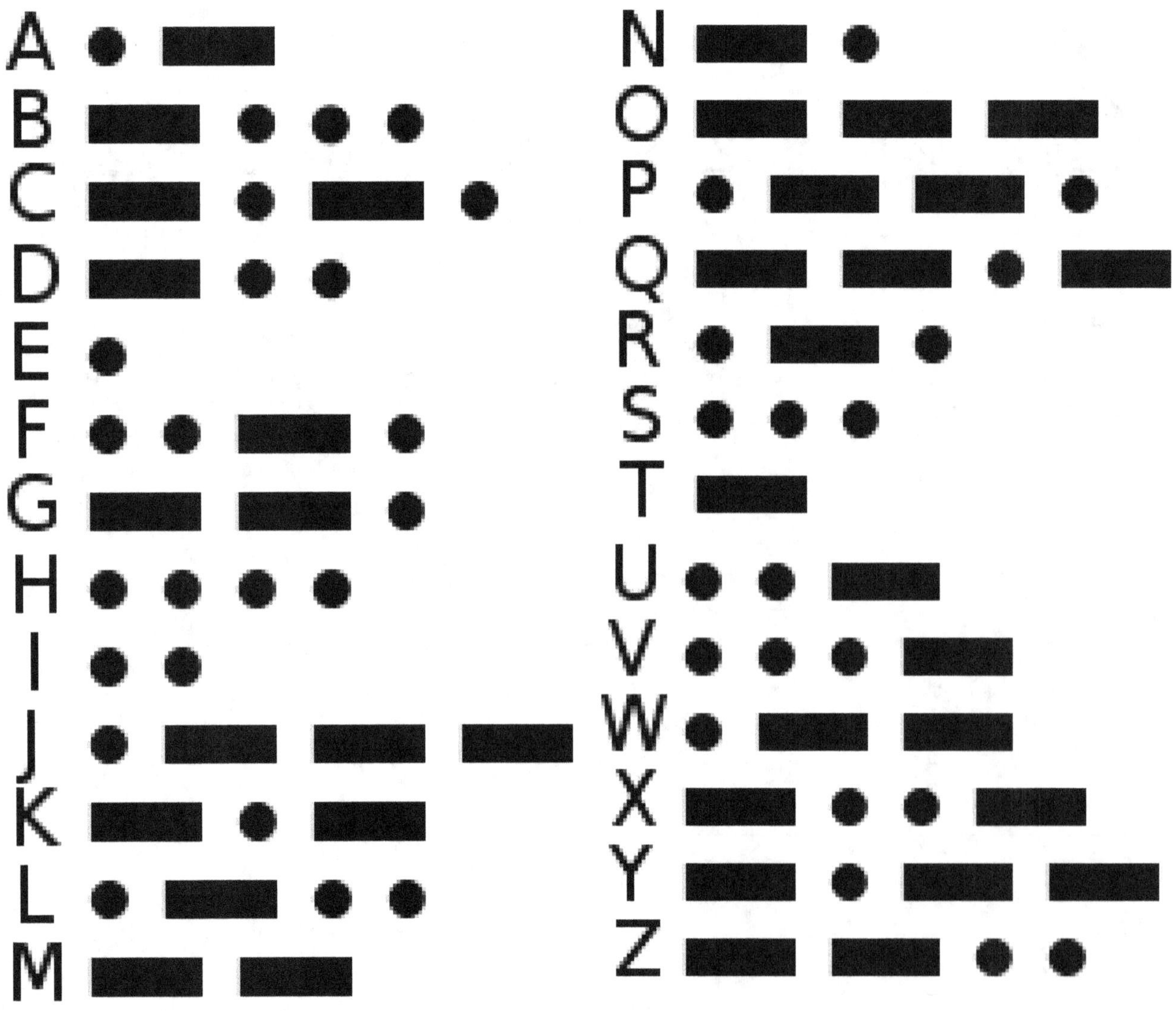

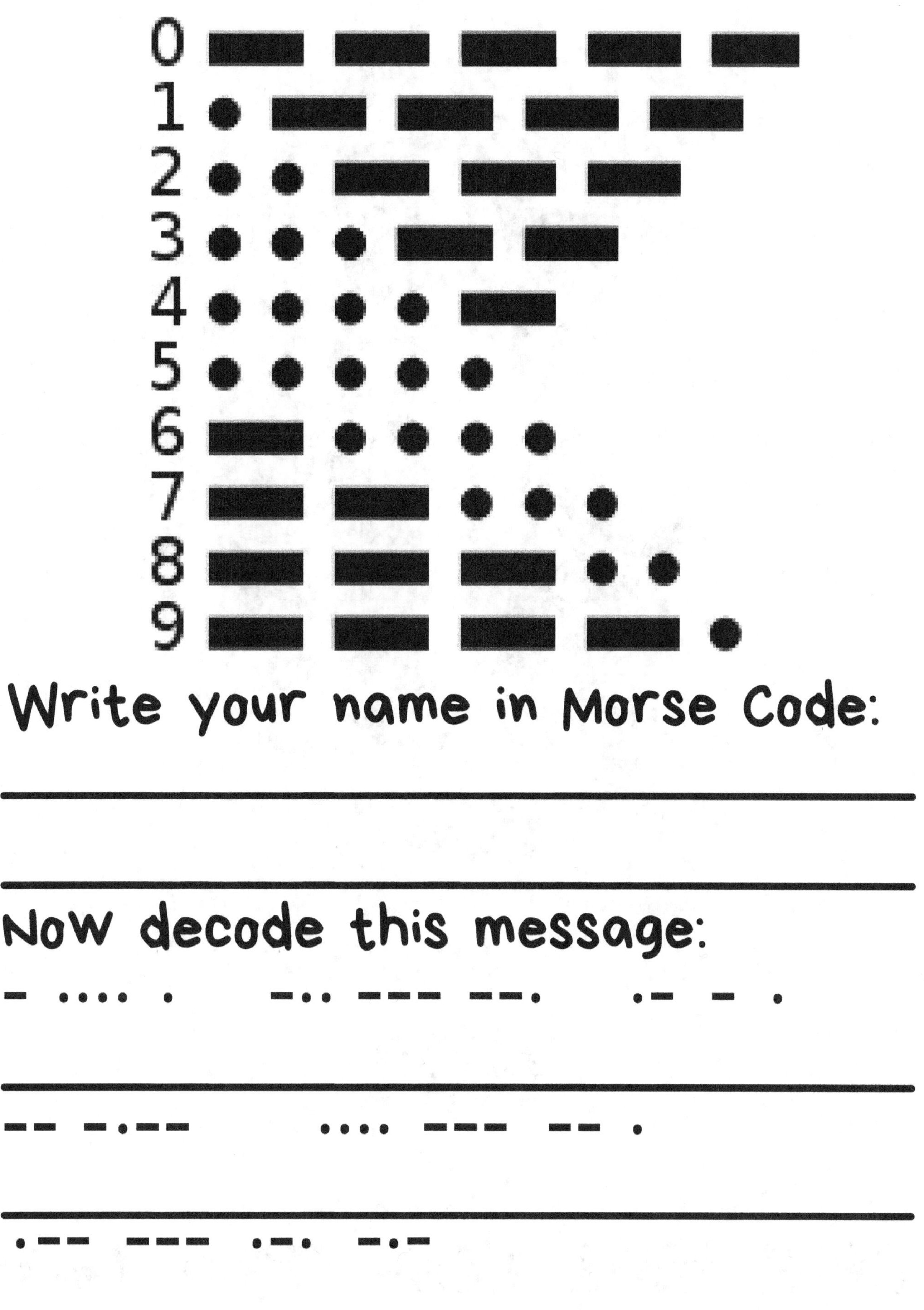

Write your name in Morse Code:

____

____

Now decode this message:

- .... .   -.. --- --. .   .- - .

____

-- -.--   .... --- -- .

____

.-- --- .-. -.-

____

ZERO

COUNT AND TRACE

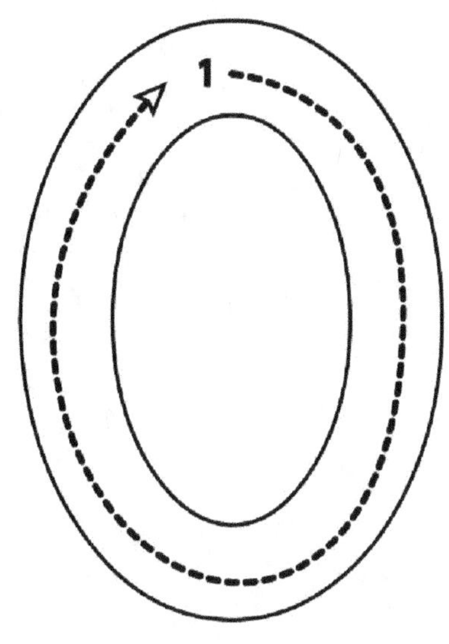

ZERO

0 0 0

0 0 0 0 0 0 0 0

0 0 0 0 0 0 0 0

zero zero zero

zero zero zero

ONE

COUNT AND TRACE

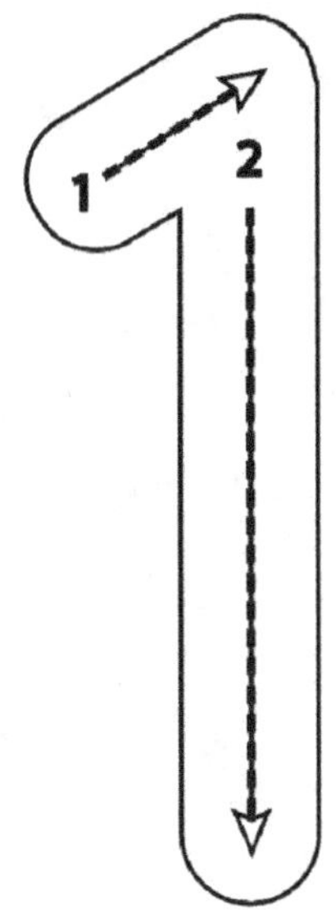

ONE

TWO

COUNT AND TRACE

2

TWO

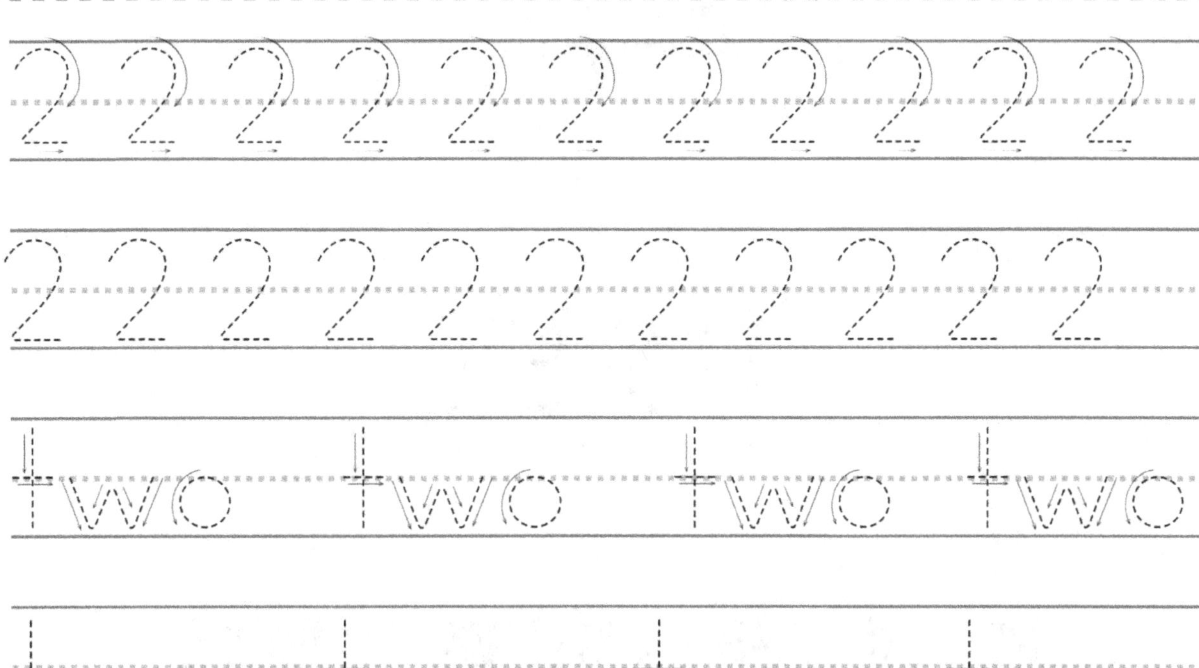

THREE

... ▬ ▬

COUNT AND TRACE

3

THREE

3 3 3

3 3 3 3 3 3 3 3 3 3 3

3 3 3 3 3 3 3 3 3 3 3

three three three

three three three

FOUR

COUNT AND TRACE

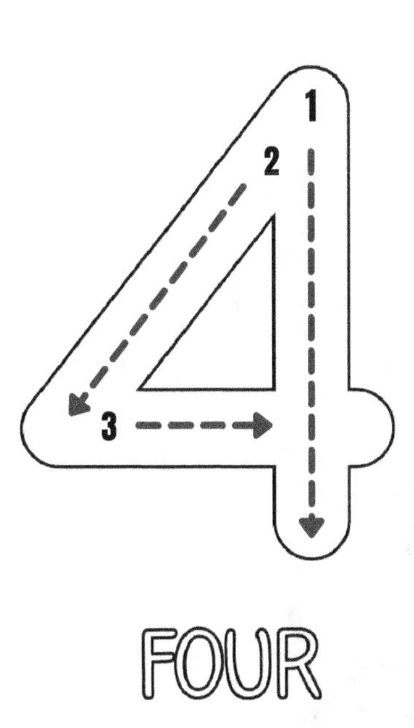

FOUR

FIVE

• • • • •

COUNT AND TRACE

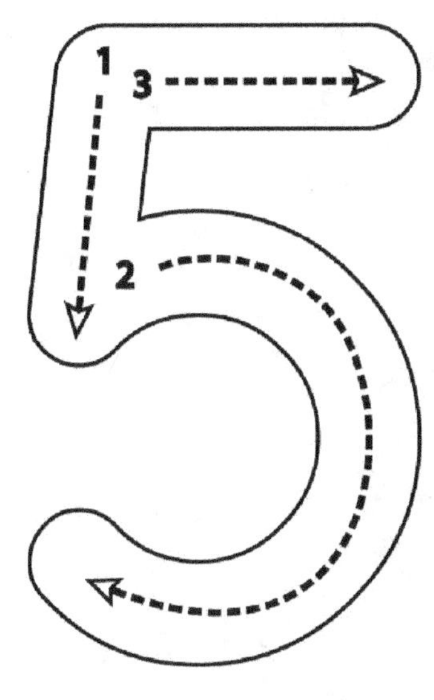

FIVE

5 5 5

5 5 5 5 5 5 5 5 5 5 5

5 5 5 5 5 5 5 5 5 5 5 5

five five five five

five five five five

SIX

COUNT AND TRACE

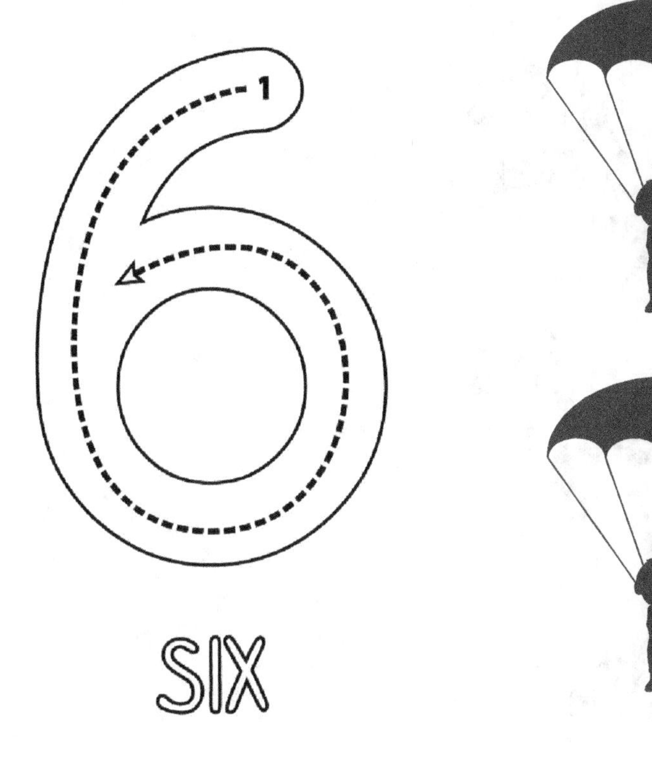

SIX

6

SEVEN

COUNT AND TRACE

7
1 → 2

SEVEN

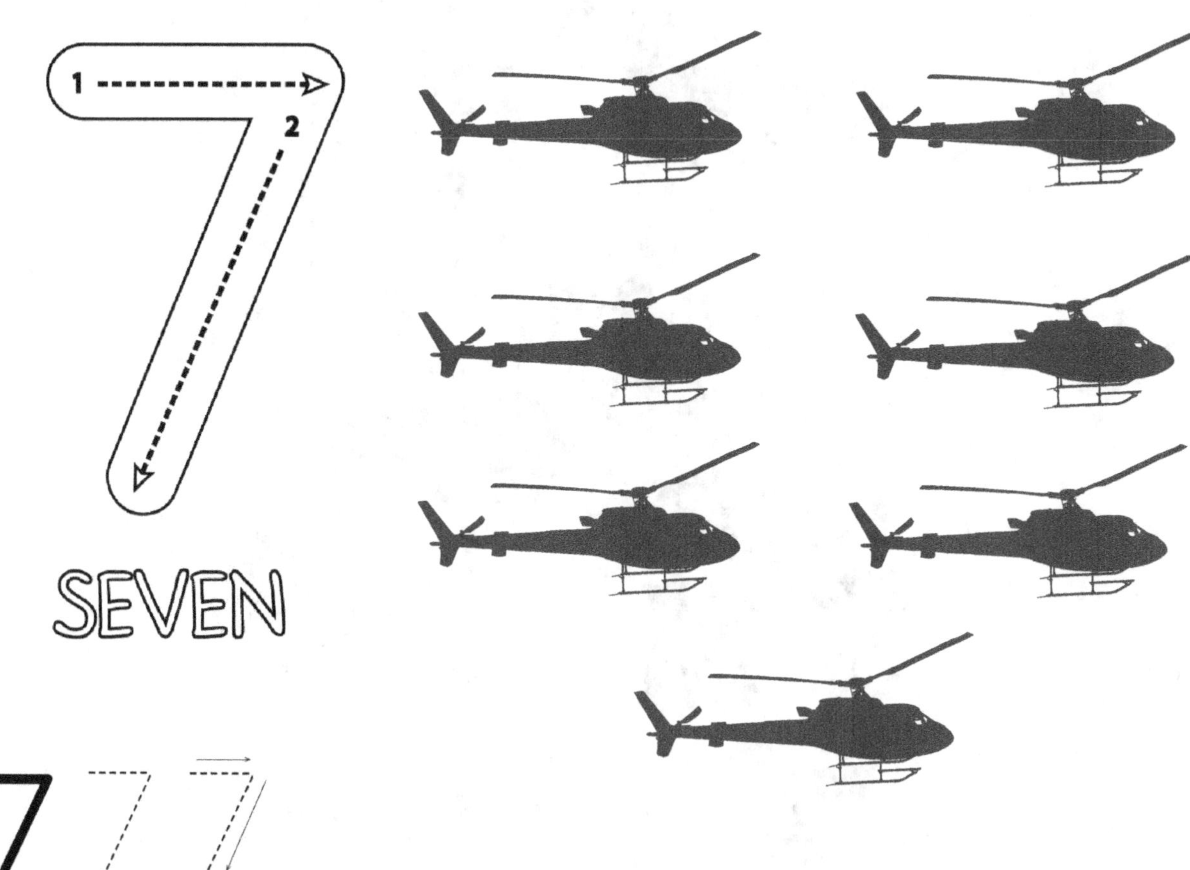

7 7 7

7 7 7 7 7 7 7 7 7 7 7 7 7

7 7 7 7 7 7 7 7 7 7 7 7

Seven Seven

seven seven seven

EIGHT

COUNT AND TRACE

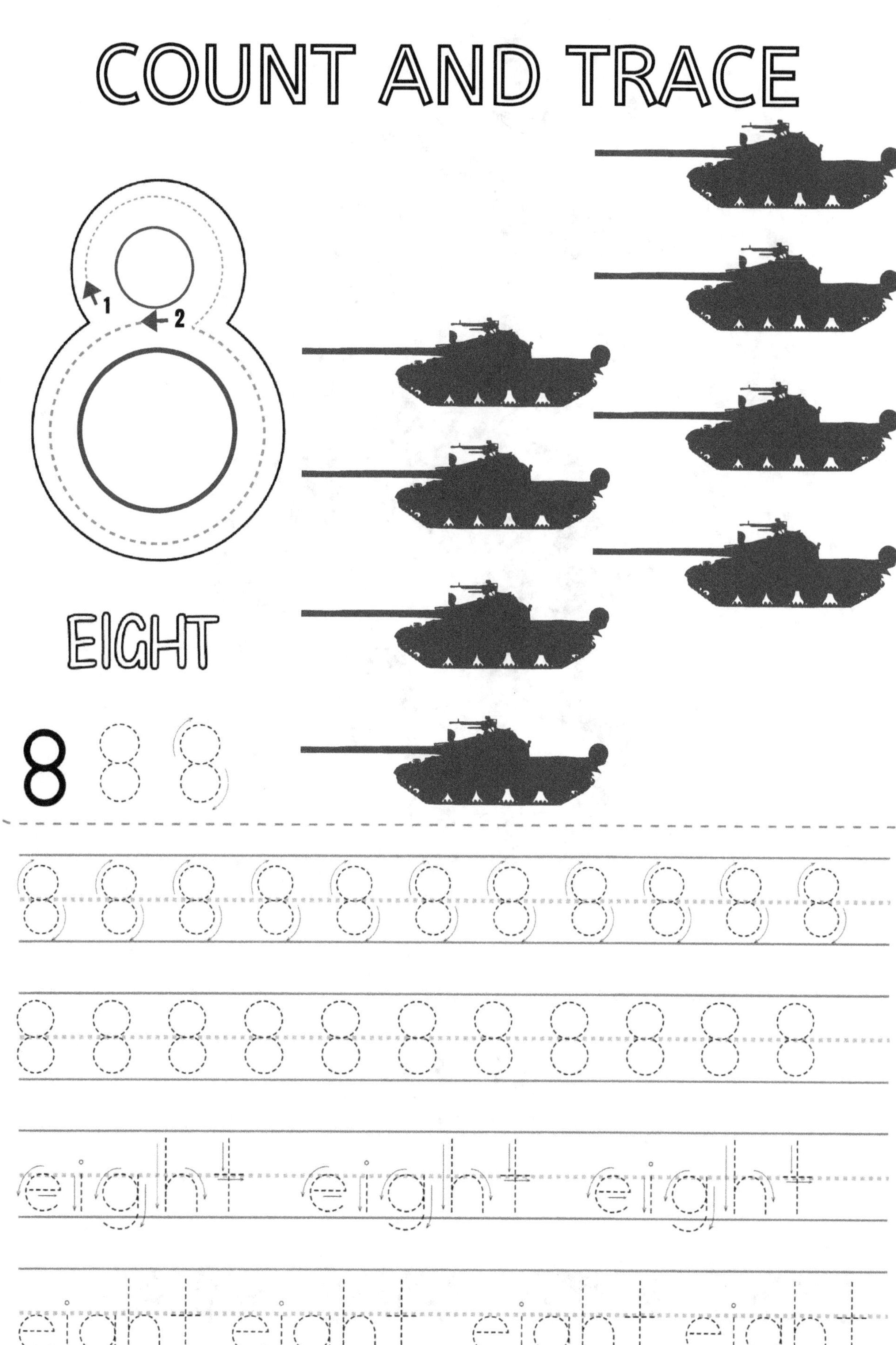

NINE

COUNT AND TRACE

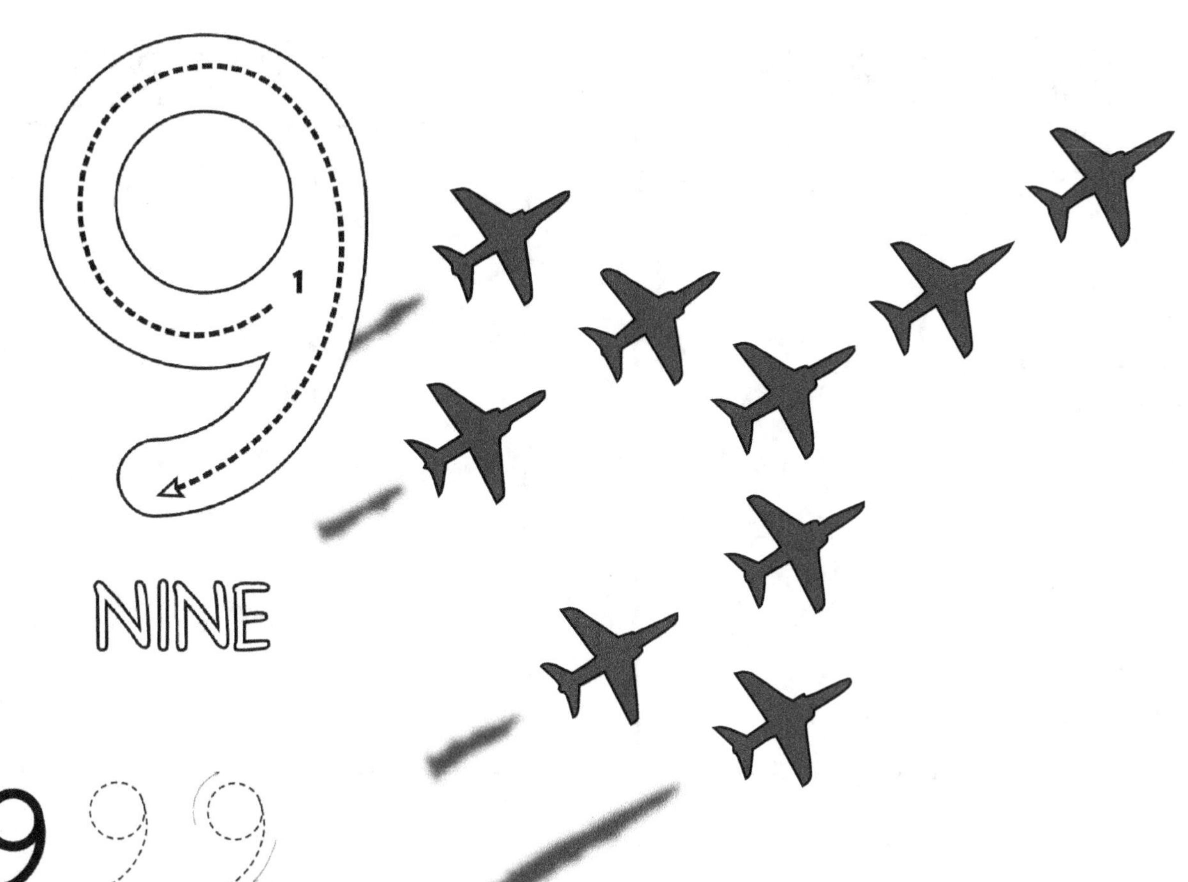

9

NINE

9 9 9

9 9 9 9 9 9 9 9 9 9 9 9 9 9

9 9 9 9 9 9 9 9 9 9 9 9 9 9

nine nine nine nine

nine nine nine nine

TRACE the PATTERN

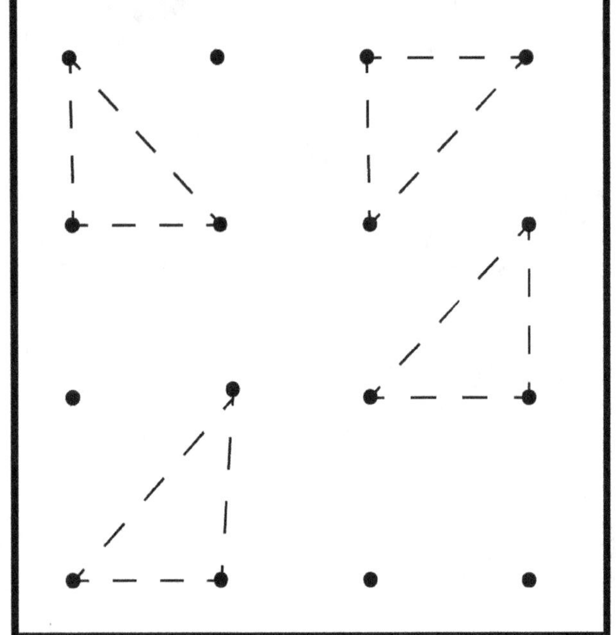

REPEAT the PATTERN

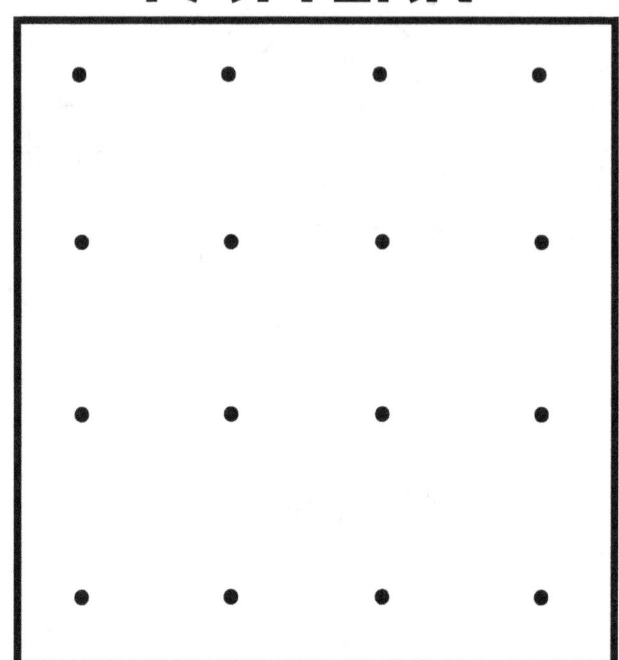

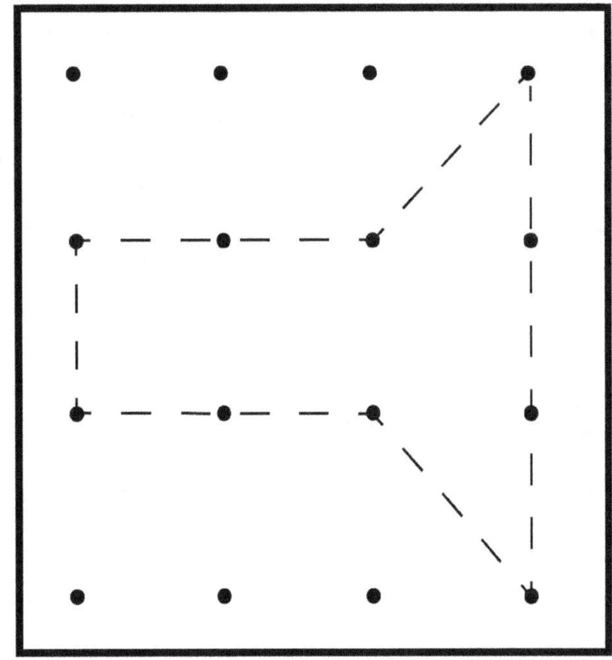

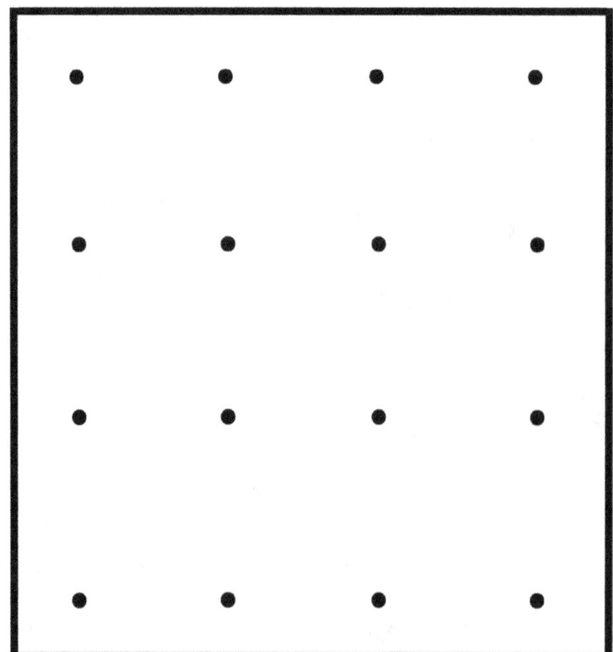

TRACE
the
PATTERN

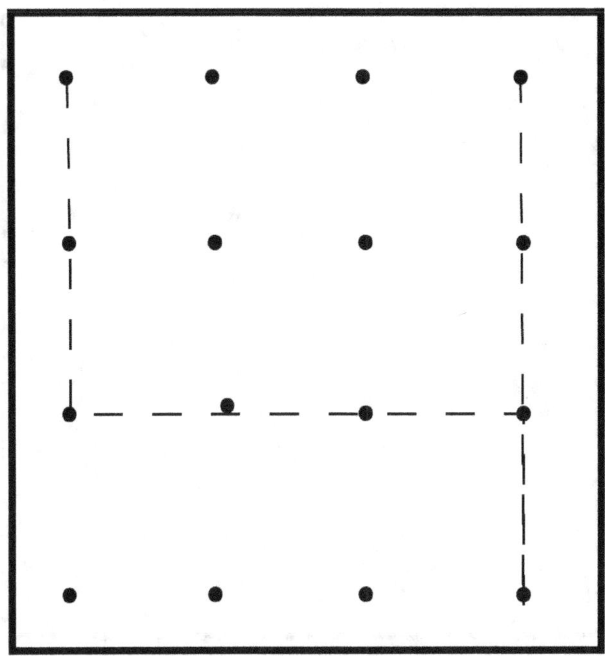

REPEAT
the
PATTERN

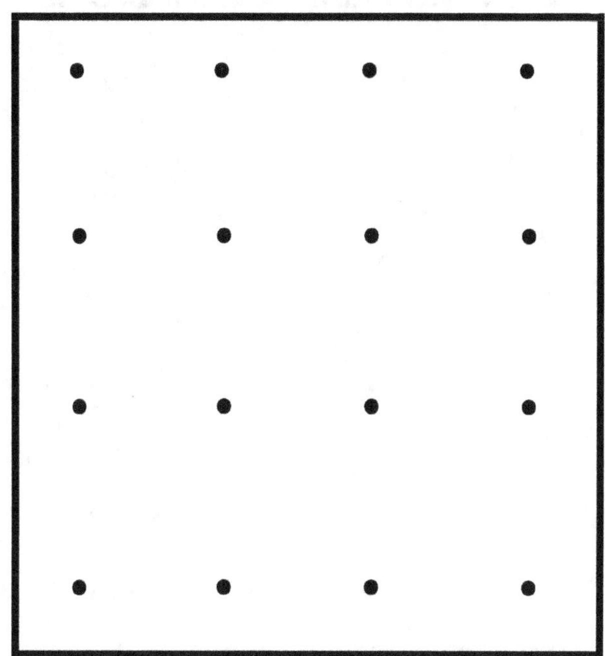

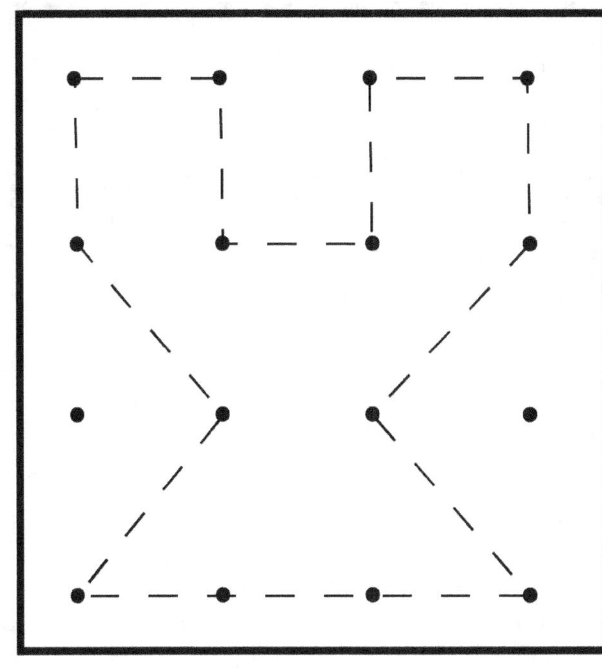

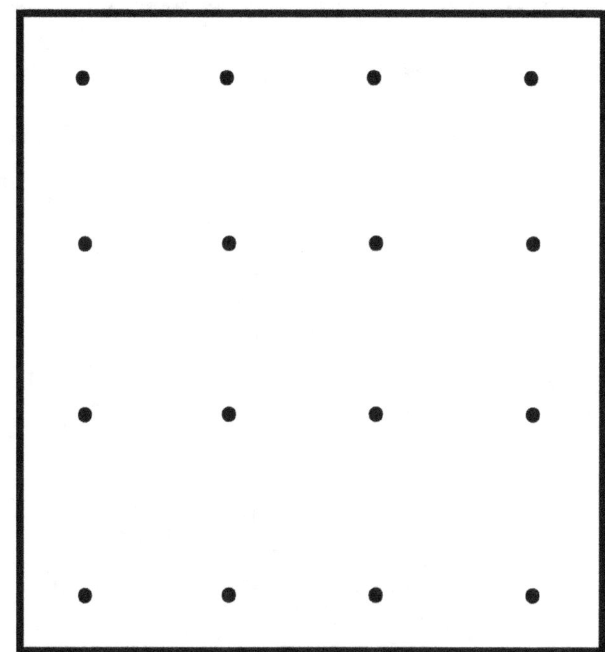

TRACE
the
PATTERN

REPEAT
the
PATTERN

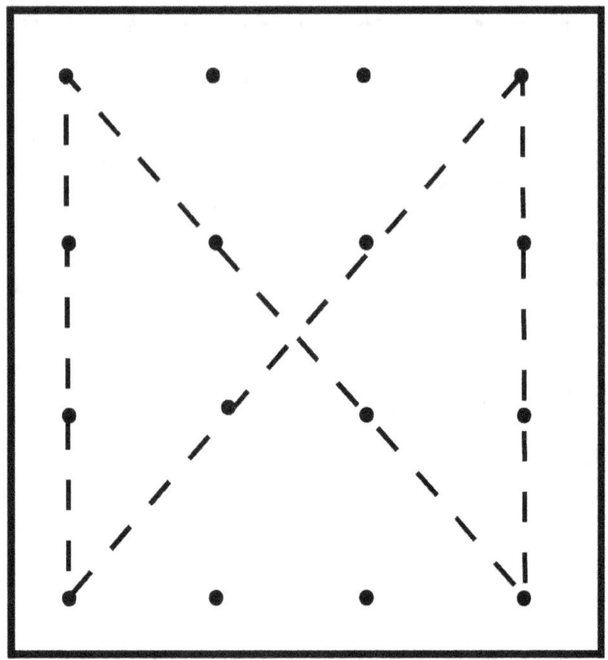

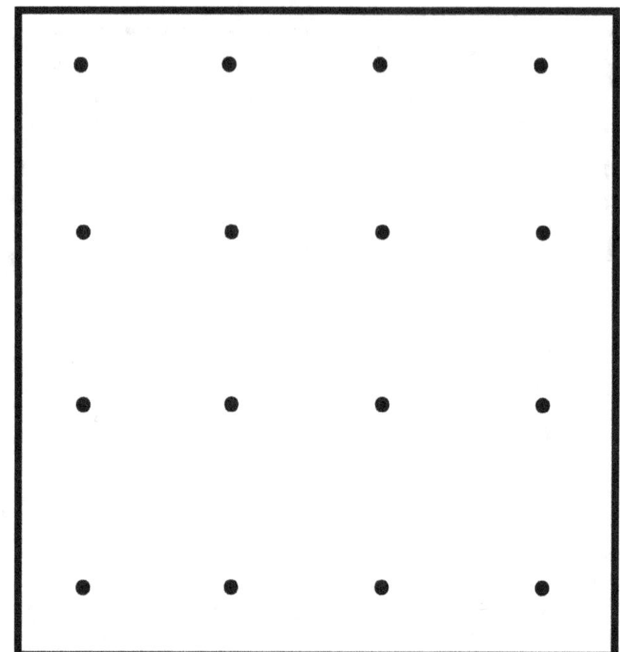

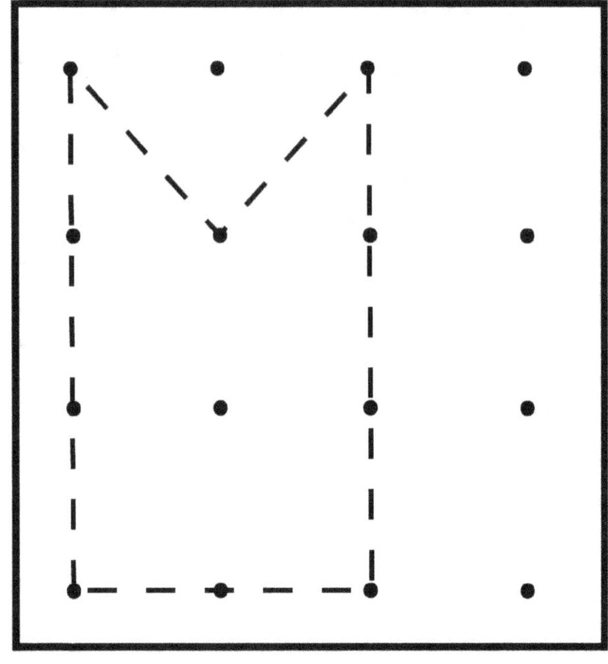

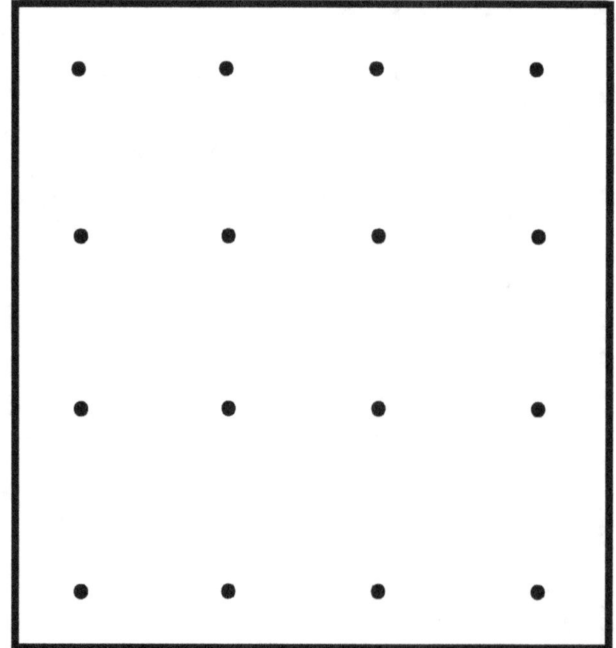

TRACE
the
PATTERN

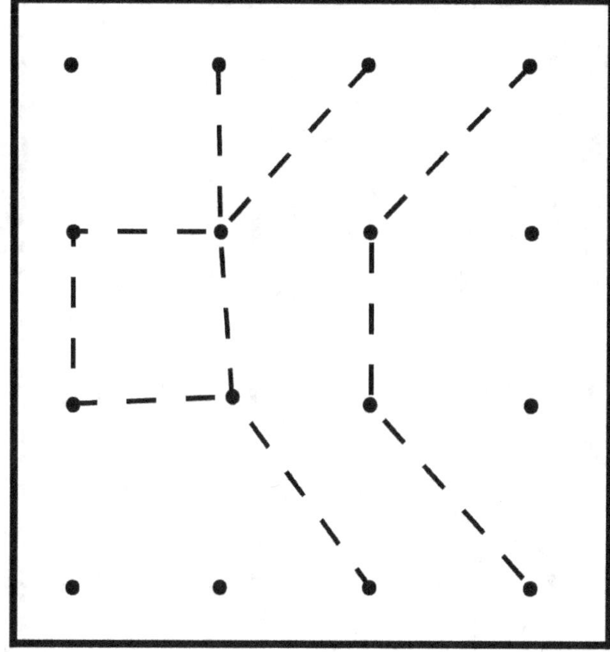

REPEAT
the
PATTERN

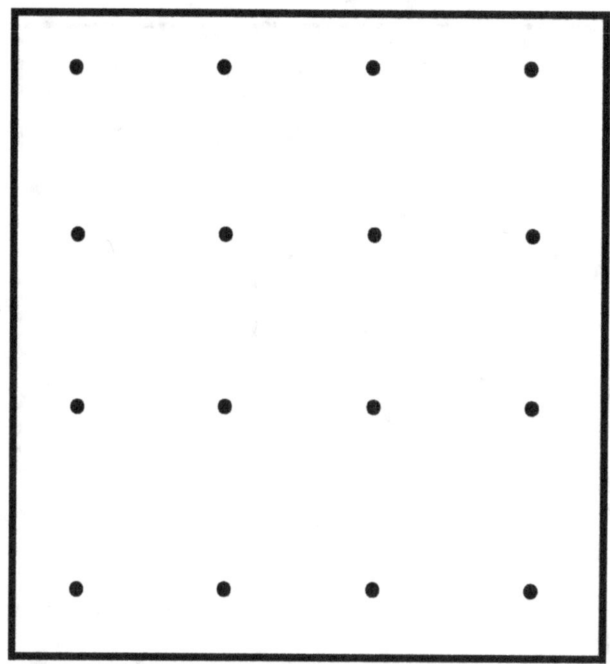

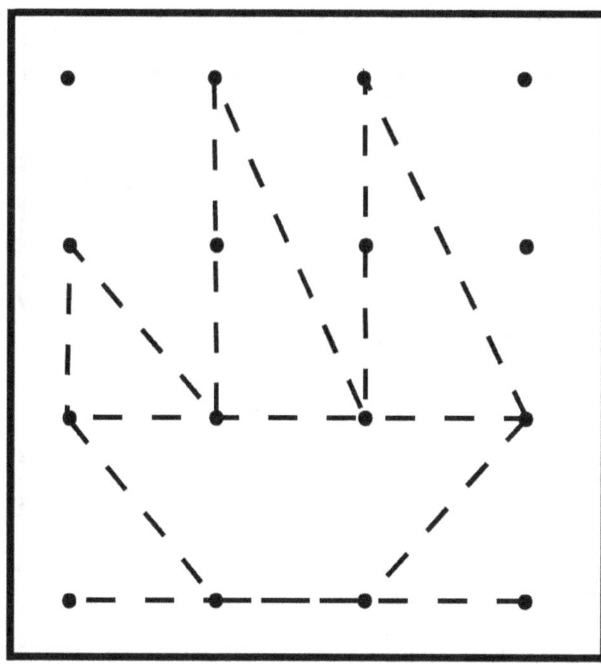

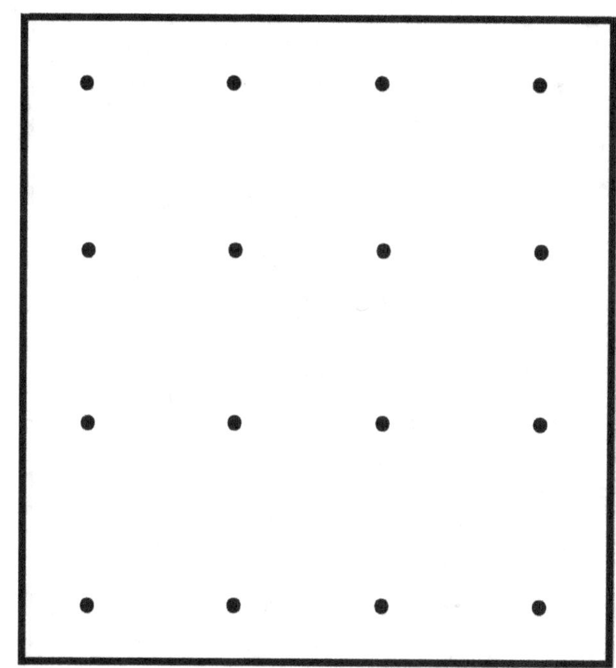

TRACE the PATTERN

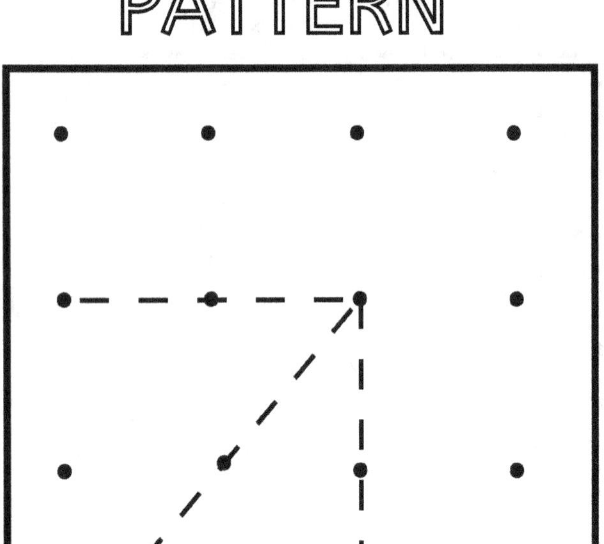

REPEAT the PATTERN

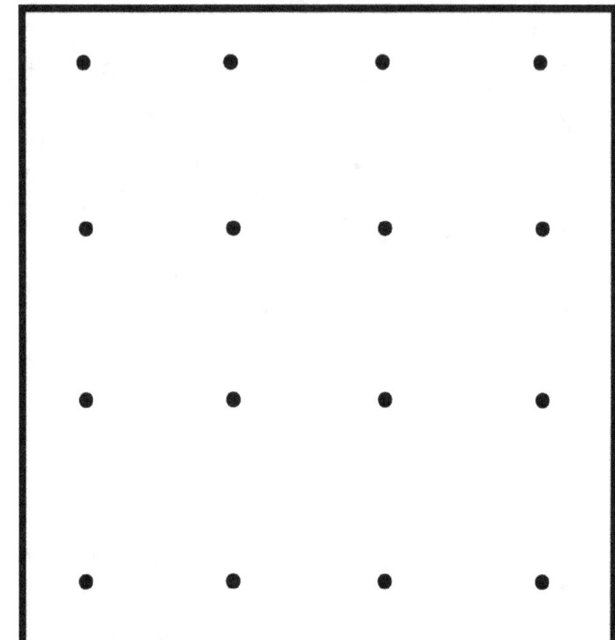

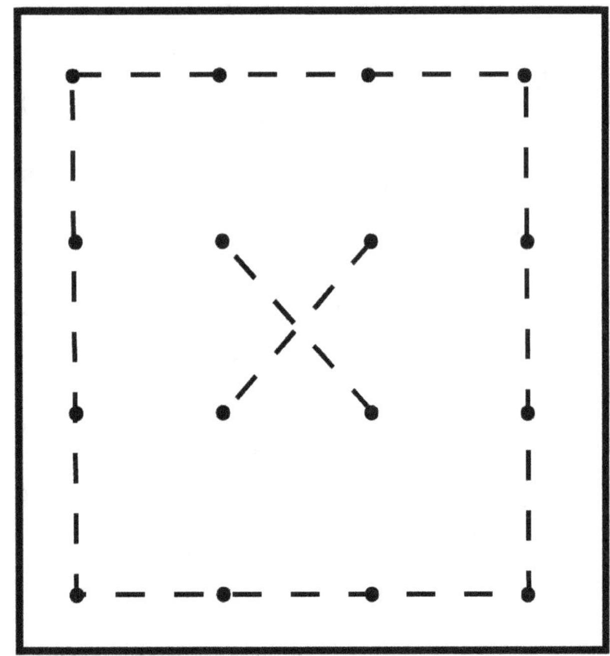

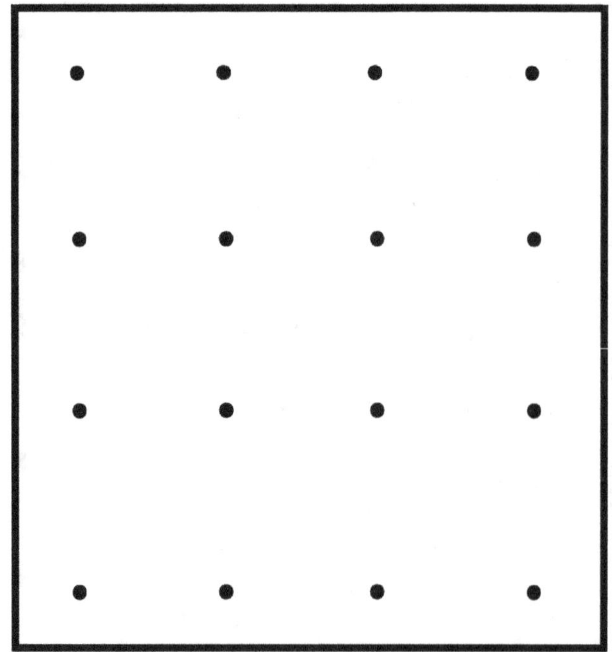

MAKE YOUR
OWN PATTERNS

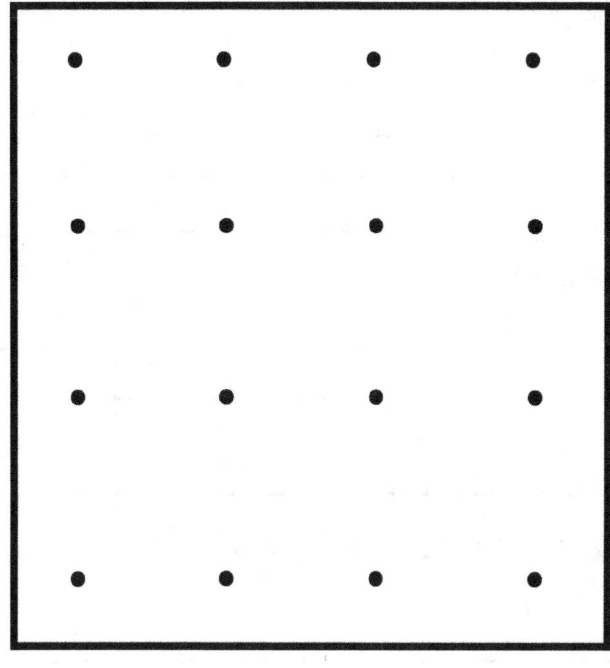

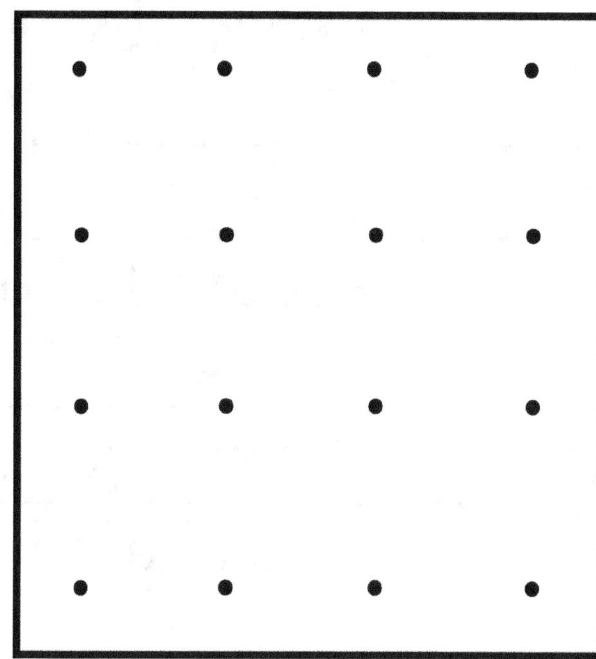

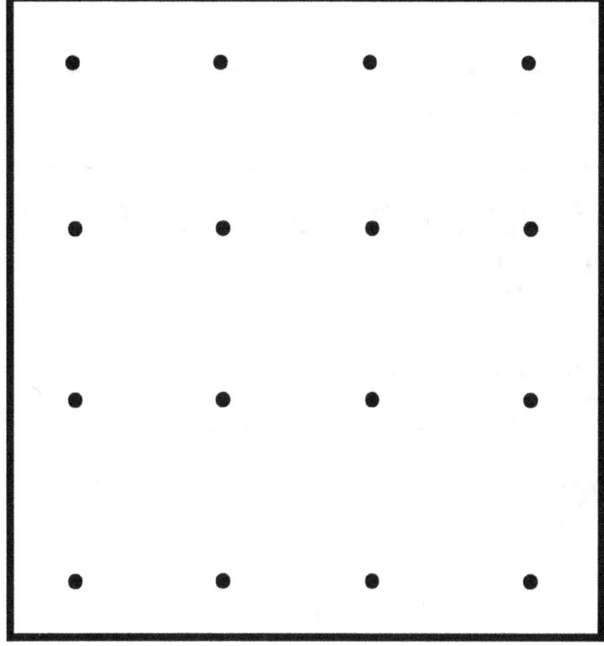

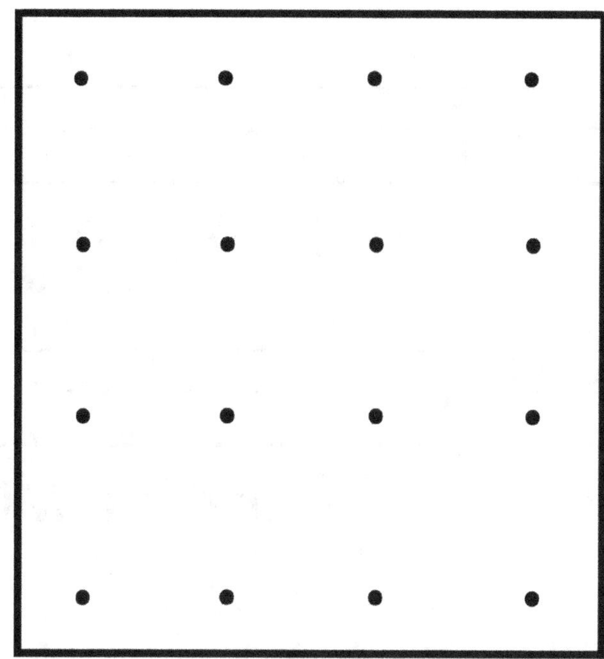

Military Slang

11 Bravo
-Army Infantry

40 Mike Mike
-Grenade Launcher

Alpha Mike Foxtrot
-Said before assaulting enemy

Bravo Zulu
-Good Job

Charlie Foxtrot
-An operation where things have gone wrong

Charlie Mike
-Continue Mission

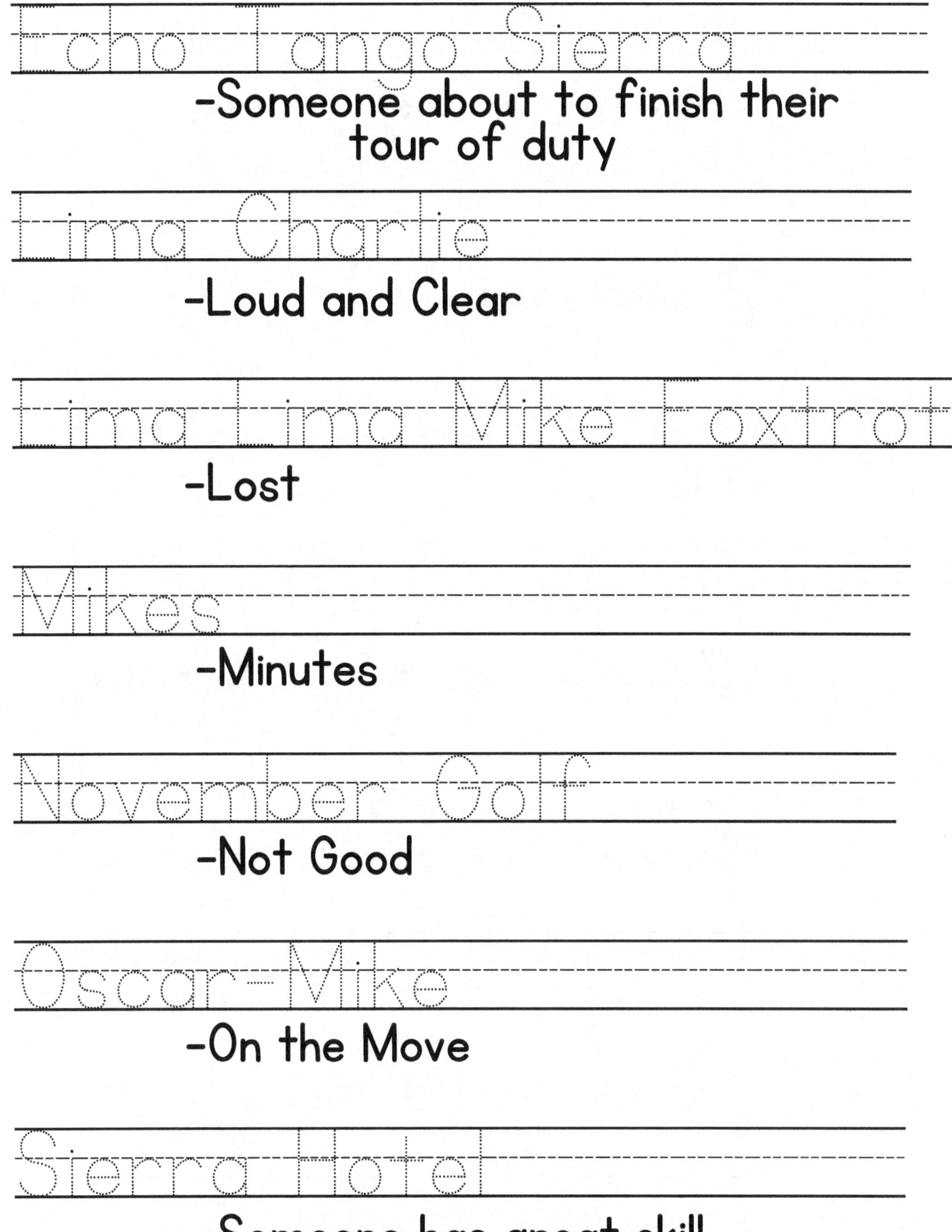

Echo Tango Sierra
-Someone about to finish their tour of duty

Lima Charlie
-Loud and Clear

Lima Lima Mike Foxtrot
-Lost

Mikes
-Minutes

November Golf
-Not Good

Oscar-Mike
-On the Move

Sierra Hotel
-Someone has great skill

Tango Delta
-Enemy was eliminated (target down)

Tango Mike
-Thanks much

Tango Yankee
-Thank you

Whiskey Charlie
-Water Closet (toilet-the head)

Whiskey Delta
-Someone who lacks courage

Let's try to memorize the military alphabet here are some tips:

A is for the ____ dog in charge.

B is another word of encouragement or Good Job.

C a name of a boy like the cartoon "_____ Brown".

D the name of an American Airline company.

E you hear this when you yell in tunnels and caves.

F a style of dance, it starts with a cute animal name.

G a sport, you hit the ball with a club so it can go into a hole.

H when you go on vacation you can stay in a ______.

I the name of a country with one of the largest world populations.

J, Shakespeare wrote a story about Romeo and _______

K a type of weight measurement.

L the capital of Peru.

M a male name, meme: everyone wants to be like ______

N, the month just before December.

N

O, a male name or if you win for best actor/actress you get an ___

O

P, some people call their father this _____

P

Q a Canadian Province.

Q

R, Shakespeare's "_______ and Juliet" play

R

S the name of a mountain range in Western United States.

S

T a great Argentinian and Uruguayan dance style.

T

U, when everyone dresses the same, they are wearing a ______.

V, when you win a game you are the ______.

W an alcoholic beverage.

X if you break a bone you get an ______

Y a term referring to people living in America.

Z an ethnic group living in South Africa.

Bee Bright
Bee Kind
Bee You

Tango Yankee

for purchasing my book, I hope it helped your child learn their ABC's. I would appreciate it if you left a Review on Amazon, it would mean a lot to my small growing business.

I have a FREE poster for you:
go to.... https://payhip.com/b/Wby7T
to upload a free Military
Alphabet Poster.

www.ingramcontent.com/pod-product-compliance
Lightning Source LLC
Chambersburg PA
CBHW081354160726
48000CB00010B/3344